On Wisdom

On Wisdom

A Philosophical Dialogue

Nicholas J. Pappas

Algora Publishing
New York

Library of Congress Cataloging-in-Publication Data —

Names: Pappas, Nicholas J., author.
Title: On wisdom / Nicholas J. Pappas.
Description: New York: Algora Publishing, 2017.
Identifiers: LCCN 2017021213| ISBN 9781628942941 (soft cover: alk. paper) | ISBN 9781628942958 (hard cover: alk. paper) | ISBN 9781628942965 (ebook)
Subjects: LCSH: Conduct of life. | Wisdom.
Classification: LCC BJ1521 .P27 2017 | DDC 158—dc23 LC record available at https://lccn.loc.gov/2017021213

Printed in the United States

Table of Contents

~ Introduction

Every word counts. Consider the title of this book. It's not called 'Wisdom'. It's called 'On Wisdom'. The 'on' opens up possibilities. 'Wisdom' suggests something more comprehensive, more definitive than what this book claims to be. This book is only one of many possible approaches to wisdom. It is limited by the characters and their setting. But most importantly, it is limited by the ability of its author. I don't doubt that it's possible to write the exhaustive treatise on wisdom. It's just not something I'd care to do, even if I could.

And who would want to read it? I think a good book should be like a letter to a very good friend. Someone you know will read every word. Accordingly, you write such a letter with a great deal of care. You craft it just so. You make every word count. Yes, this will take more time than writing at greater length in a rambling way. But even though your words will likely take less time to read, there's a good chance they'll be read or remembered again and again – and provide food for thought, for the heart.

I'd like to look at the whole of a chapter of this book and make a few comments. The chapter is "Rarity." It begins thus:

Artist: Wisdom is necessarily rare.

Director: You mean everyone can't be wise?

Artist: Yes, it's like it is at the races. Not all the horses can win.

Sage: But wisdom isn't about competing.

Heir: What's it about?

Sage: Choosing wisely and living well.

Artist: And everyone can choose wisely and live well?

Sage: That's my belief. Why? Do you believe the world is a zero sum game? If I do well someone else must do poorly?

Artist doesn't say wisdom is rare. He says wisdom is necessarily rare. It's in the nature of wisdom to be rare. And that's because wisdom is essentially competitive. As there are horses of varying swiftness, there are people of varying degrees of wisdom, only a few of which come out on top.

Sage rejects this view. To him, wisdom is about choice. We can choose to be wise. We can make wise choices which lead to living well. Choice is not necessarily competitive. There's nothing in my choosing well that stops you from choosing well.

We continue:

Artist: No, I don't believe that. Not absolutely. But I think you're naive about this, Sage.

Sage: How so?

Artist: Being wise gives you an advantage over others. If everyone is wise, that advantage disappears. And then what's the point of wisdom?

Sage: Artist, it's as I said. Wisdom is for the sake of living well.

Artist appears to soften his view. He now declares wisdom is about advantage. If there is to be advantage, wisdom must be relatively rare. Why the shift? And how great a shift is it to go from winning to advantage? Doesn't advantage allow you to win?

Sage, feeling his advantage, repeats himself. Wisdom is for living well. But doesn't advantage allow you to live well?

Then Heir steps in:

Heir: I think Sage is right.

Heir sides with Sage. Is that because he, too, senses the advantage in taking this line? Why not side with Artist? From elsewhere in the book we see that Heir has every advantage. Money, position, intelligence, looks. But does he see these as signs of his wisdom? Perhaps he feels he must choose to use his advantages well. Perhaps Sage can teach him how. What can Artist teach?

Artist: Yes, yes. But that only confirms that the wise have always been few. Not many live well, you know.

Artist enlists Sage's point in order to prove his own. He knows Heir lives well, very well — at least by most people's standards. And he believes Heir sees there are many who don't live well, however defined.

But Heir won't let him leave it at that:

Heir: Oh, I don't know. More might live well than we think.

Artist: Ha! And why do you think that?

Heir politely disagrees. And Artist laughs. Why does he laugh? Does he believe Heir is dissembling? Or does he think Heir is naive, as he said of Sage? In any case, he asks Heir why. And Heir tells him:

Heir: Because who's to judge who truly lives well?

Is this a moral stand by Heir? Who of us is to judge another? Or is it a democratic platitude? (Heir is running for office.) Then again, could this be the kernel of wisdom itself, the most basic wisdom there is? Wise ones don't judge?

Director chimes in:

Director: But don't we all have to judge this to the best of our knowledge?

Director stops the talk about 'wise ones'. All of us have to judge, wise and unwise alike. But he doesn't state this outright. He asks a question, one leaning toward the answer 'yes', but a question nonetheless. So we ask ourselves — do we need to judge? We are compelled to wonder what life would be like without judging how others live.

But Heir asks:

Heir: Why would you say that?

Heir doesn't say, 'Why do you think that?', or, 'Is that true?' He says why would you 'say' that. Is Heir chiding Director for saying something impolitic? Or is he truly wondering about Director's reasons? We can't tell from this chapter alone. But we can consider that he might be questioning his own opinion. So, we wonder. Does Heir secretly judge others and lie about it? Or does he refuse to judge but now questions if that's good?

Sage concludes:

Sage: I know why. Because we all hope to live well, and we long for examples of what this means.

Sage claims to know Director's mind. And he gives a plausible reason for why he thinks he knows Director's mind. Our minds are all the same in the most important regard—everyone hopes to live well. But is that true? Do we all have hope? And if we do, do we all hope for the same things? If not, how can our minds all be the same?

Sage speaks of longing for examples. We judge the examples that come before us. We judge if they live well. Which is to say, we need to know what living well means before we can judge. Sage doesn't appear to see the difficulty. Or he assumes the examples will teach us what living well means.

***

The above shows some of my considerations as I write, some of the questions I ask myself. Undoubtedly, there are many more questions and concerns that I blindly ignore. But I intend to keep on learning.

Happy reading.

Nick Pappas

~ Wisdom (Artist, Director, Heir, Sage)

Heir: Welcome to the party! Director, Artist, this is Sage.

Artist: Ah, the man we've heard so much about.

Sage: It's a pleasure to meet you both.

Director: It's a pleasure to meet you. Heir tells us you're an adviser.

Sage: Yes, I am.

Artist: And he tells us you don't charge for your services.

Sage: It's true.

Director: He says you practice informally. What does that mean?

Sage: I haven't got any formal training. I simply offer people advice.

Artist: And you offered Heir advice?

Sage: Yes, I did.

Artist: What advice?

Sage: That's not for me to say. But he can tell you, if he likes.

Heir: I'd rather not.

Artist: Was it good advice?

Heir: Very good.

Artist: Then Sage must be wise.

Heir: Oh, don't be sarcastic, Artist.

Artist: Sarcastic? But I believe Sage seems wise.

Director: Sage, do you believe you're wise?

Sage: It's not a matter of belief, Director. I know I am, at least to some extent.

Director: Then maybe we can chat a bit, and you can share with us a little of what you know. But for now, I'd like a word with Heir.

~ What, How (Artist, Sage)

Artist: Do you ever feel like a fool when you give advice?

Sage: Why would I?

Artist: Because your advisees don't always listen. Do they?

Sage: No, not always. But why would that make me a fool?

Artist: Because you should know what to say to get them to listen.

Sage: If they won't listen to wisdom, I don't know what they'll listen to.

Artist: Yes, yes. But don't you know about seasoning?

Sage: What do you mean?

Artist: You spice what you have to say with how you say it.

Sage: Ah, you're talking about substance and style. But sometimes the wisdom I share is best said in just a few words.

Artist: Then your style is terse. Or you find a way to employ more than just a few words.

Sage: But why would I do that? Wouldn't those words be empty?

Artist: Good 'how' is never empty.

Sage: Yes, good 'how' is tasty spice. I understand. But how good is it if I use much more spice than meat?

Artist: Oh, forget that metaphor. Better yet, reverse it.

Sage: 'How' is the meat and 'what' is the spice?

Artist: Yes.

Sage: Now you're just being ridiculous.

Artist: Really? Ha! Then let's be truly ridiculous. Both are meat and spice at once.

Sage: So 'what' adds flavor to 'how', just as 'how' adds flavor to 'what'?

Artist: Of course! And that's how it should be — if you hope to compel others by making an art of what you say.

~ Belief (Director, Sage)

Director: Ah, Sage. Here you are. There's something I've been wondering. Would you say Heir believes in you?

Sage: Yes, Director, I would.

Director: Would it be more precise to say he believes in your wisdom?

Sage: I don't see how. Wisdom is inseparable from the one who's wise.

Director: Does that mean all of you is wise?

Sage: I'd say wisdom is my most important part.

Director: But then there are parts of you that aren't wise?

Sage: Yes, but I don't see what you're getting at.

Director: Do you think Heir knows of your less than wise parts?

Sage: Why are you asking?

Director: Because I think he needs to know you're human.

Sage: Ha, ha. Heir certainly knows that.

Director: How?

Sage: He's no fool.

Director: I agree. But he's young. And don't the young sometimes idealize those they believe in?

Sage: True. So what would you have me do?

Director: Show him freely you're not simply wise.

Sage: And if he interprets that as a wise thing to do?

Director: Tell him why it's not.

Sage: And if he takes what I say to be yet another sign of wisdom?

Director: Then I think you need some practice — in how not to seem so wise.

~ Strength (Director, Heir, Sage)

Director: Can you be wise but weak, or is wisdom a sort of strength?

Sage: A very good question. Let me put it this way. You might be wise but not have the strength to carry out what your wisdom tells you needs to be done.

Director: But shouldn't your wisdom tell you to do what lies within your strength? I mean, is it wise to tell myself to lift ten thousand pounds when I know I can't?

Sage: Well, of course not. Wisdom should know what's possible.

Director: So you should always have the strength to do what wisdom tells you to do?

Sage: Yes.

Director: Then it's not that wisdom is a strength. It's that wisdom understands your strength, and knows what to do with it.

Sage: I think that's fair to say.

Heir: And when you're weak, your wisdom knows you're weak?

Sage: Yes, Heir, it does.

Heir: But then it would tell you to build yourself up. Right?

Sage: Yes and no. There are times when it's wise to be weak.

Director: That's hard to believe. Can you tell us how so?

Sage: Of course. Here's an example. Suppose you have very little free time. In that time you can either lift weights or read books written by the wise. You can't do both.

Heir: So what would you do?

Sage: I'd read and make my mind strong. But then my muscles would be weak. That's the point.

Director: Yes, but I question your emphasis, Sage. If you choose one strength over another, you shouldn't say: 'It's wise to be weak.' You should say: 'It's wise to be strong in what you think best.'

Heir: I agree. And what I think best right now is to be a strong host! So tell me at the end of the party — whether you think I'm wise.

~ Weakness (Artist, Heir)

Artist: Certain weaknesses are desirable.

Heir: Can you name one?

Artist: A weakness for fine wine.

Heir: But is that really a weakness? Isn't that just good taste?

Artist: Sure. But if I'm down to my last dollars, and I can't resist spending them all on a very good bottle of red, how good is my taste then?

Heir: Your taste is excellent — because it's best to go down in style!

Artist: Ha! I knew there was a reason I liked you.

Heir: Let's name another desirable weakness. Do you have any others?

Artist: I do. A weakness for good friends.

Heir: And how is that a weakness?

Artist: I give in and spend time at play with my friends when I should be doing something else.

Heir: Like working your craft?

Artist: Yes. And it gets complicated, Heir. Because, as you might have guessed, I have a weakness for my work.

Heir: Sometimes you work when you should be playing with friends?

Artist: Two opposed weaknesses. Yes.

Heir: Well, here's where it gets interesting — because two opposed weaknesses can make a strength!

Artist: You think so? I'm tempted to agree! But how do they make a strength?

Heir: When you forget about 'should' and do whichever thing you like, when you like, you're fresh. And when you're fresh, you thrive. And when you thrive, you're strong.

Artist: Ah, I like your formula! So what's the opposing weakness to my weakness for fine wine? Can someone actually have a weakness for... sobriety?

- Unbelief (Artist, Director, Heir, Sage)

Artist: Unbelief is the greatest form of wisdom.

Heir: Why would you say that?

Artist: Because when you believe you can be fooled. But you're never fooled when you don't believe.

Sage: Oh, I don't believe that. Unbelief can be a sort of belief, one that can fool you, one that might cause you to miss out on something good, something worth believing in.

Artist: If it's truly something good, it's worth knowing, not believing in.

Sage: So you would never allow yourself the delight of belief?

Artist: The delight of belief? Ha! Is that what wisdom amounts to?

Sage: Wisdom amounts to knowing what to believe in and what not to believe in.

Artist: And how can you tell the one from the other?

Sage: The things to believe in are good for you.

Artist: And how do you know what's good for you?

Sage: Don't we all know that, Artist?

Artist: Director, you're going to have to help me here.

Director: Sage, you're saying we somehow simply know what's good for us. Yes?

Sage: Yes.

Director: And it never happens that we believe a belief is good but have it wrong?

Sage: Well, of course that happens. But next time we'll be all the wiser.

Director: And by wiser we mean we've learned what's good for us?

Sage: Yes.

Director: And when we learn, we know? Or do we believe we know?

Sage: We know. And yes, it's better to know than to believe — in order to know what to believe, for all those things we can never know.

- Religion (Artist, Director, Heir, Sage)

Sage: Religion needs wisdom in order to flourish.

Director: I've heard otherwise. But you're saying if the wise abandon religion, religion declines?

Sage: Yes.

Director: And when the wise abandon religion, where do they go?

Sage: More often than not? To science.

Director: Does that make science a sort of religion?

Sage: Yes, in a way — or at least a substitute for religion.

Director: And if the wise abandon science, will science decline?

Sage: Absolutely.

Heir: But if the wise abandon science, where do they go?

Sage: Some go back to religion.

Artist: And the rest?

Sage: They're in limbo.

Heir: Where they await the new religion?

Artist: Why do they need a new religion?

Heir: Because they need something to fill the void.

Artist: But you don't need religion for that. Just do what I do — have faith in yourself and your work. That fills any void.

Heir: But then that faith is your religion. No?

Sage: Yes, and I think many of us partake in this belief. Director, don't you agree?

Director: I agree many of us do. But why does it seem to me the religion of self and work rings increasingly hollow?

Sage: Because so many of its believers have nothing inside.

- Secularism (Director, Sage)

Director: Sage, tell me. Where do we find more wisdom? In things secular or things religious?

Sage: Religious in the old sense? Well, all I can say is that I only give secular advice.

Director: Why?

Sage: Because I have no religious wisdom to offer.

Director: But you believe there are those who do have religious wisdom to offer?

Sage: Yes, of course.

Director: What's the nature of their wisdom?

Sage: It's... religious.

Director: Religious as in serves the soul?

Sage: Yes, but secular wisdom can do that, too.

Director: Then how is religious wisdom different than secular wisdom?

Sage: It has to do with things eternal.

Director: You mean to say secular wisdom can't partake in eternal truth?

Sage: No, that's not what I mean to say.

Director: Then how is it? How do the two wisdoms differ?

Sage: One has to do with this life and the other has largely to do with the next, in some religions at least.

Director: Which is to say those religions don't have much to do with this life?

Sage: I think someone wise in these matters would say this life is the key to the next.

Director: And someone wise in secular matters would say this life is the key... to this life?

Sage: Yes.

Director: Then in either case, this life is key.

~ Spirit (Artist, Heir)

Artist: Heir, would you say you're wise in spiritual matters?

Heir: No, I wouldn't.

Artist: Why not?

Heir: They don't interest me.

Artist: What? They don't interest you? What could be more important than the spirit?

Heir: Spiritual matters and the spirit aren't the same thing.

Artist: What do you mean?

Heir: The spirit — as in the fighting spirit, for instance — is a physical thing.

Artist: Ha!

Heir: Why do you laugh?

Artist: Because that's my opinion, too.

Heir: And is it your opinion that spiritual matters are immaterial?

Artist: Yes, of course, in a sense.

Heir: Well, you know, many won't believe us that the spirit is physical.

Artist: Oh, I don't know. Advances in medical sciences should make that clear enough to everyone soon.

Heir: But what if people don't want to believe it?

Artist: Seeing is believing.

Heir: Yes, but not everyone is willing to see what science would have them see.

Artist: Then I suppose some will believe spirit is immaterial.

Heir: What harm do you think there is in that?

Artist: What harm? What harm is there in thinking something isn't physical when it is?

Heir: I don't know. But I bet if we look hard enough we'll see.

- Practical (Artist, Heir)

Heir: Do you think all wisdom is practical?

Artist: 'Is' or 'should be'?

Heir: Should be.

Artist: Yes, I think all wisdom should be practical.

Heir: Can we even call something wisdom if it's not practical?

Artist: Can we? I don't. But there are those who do.

Heir: Why do you think they do that?

Artist: Impractical 'wisdom' sometimes tells them what they want to hear.

Heir: And what do they want to hear?

Artist: Ha! What do any of us want to hear?

Heir: That it's going to be alright.

Artist: Well, Heir, there are those who will tell us that it's going to be alright when it won't.

Heir: Why won't it be alright?

Artist: Because we're not doing what we need to do.

Heir: We're not being practical.

Artist: Yes.

Heir: But what practical things do we need to do?

Artist: There's only one. We need to take charge of our lives.

Heir: Why don't we all take charge?

Artist: We're afraid.

Heir: Of what?

Artist: The responsibility that comes with being in control.

- Doubts (Heir, Sage)

Heir: Sage, is it wise to doubt?

Sage: Some of the greatest wisdom comes from doubts.

Heir: But what if we doubt everything?

Sage: Some of the greatest wisdom comes from doubting everything.

Heir: But we can't live in total doubt, can we?

Sage: I think there are those who can.

Heir: I don't believe it.

Sage: Well, yes. There are moments when we can live in total doubt. But not all the time.

Heir: But why did you change your opinion? Was it for my sake? You say there are those who can live in total doubt, and then you say it's only for moments. Which is it?

Sage: Those moments seem like a lifetime, Heir. That's the sense I mean.

Heir: And what do people learn in that 'lifetime' of doubt?

Sage: That not everything is what it seems.

Heir: And that's what wisdom is?

Sage: A part of wisdom.

Heir: What's the other part?

Sage: Knowing that things are sometimes what they seem.

Heir: So how can you tell the things that are what they seem from the things that aren't?

Sage: It takes practice.

Heir: Which means you'll make mistakes?

Sage: Of course. But you learn from your mistakes.

Heir: Then I suppose that's the wisest thing you can do.

~ Creation (Artist, Director)

Artist: If we want to succeed, we must clear up our doubts.

Director: We must be certain.

Artist: Yes.

Director: And when we're certain what must we do?

Artist: We must act.

Director: Act? How so?

Artist: What do you mean, 'How so?'

Director: I mean, must we act the way you act?

Artist: And how do I act?

Director: You create

Artist: Ha! Yes. That's how we all must act.

Director: So we all must be artists?

Artist: Artists of life, yes.

Director: And our works are marred if they're made with doubt?

Artist: Of course they are.

Director: But tell me this. What if we're certain when it comes to our creations but doubt all things else? Possible?

Artist: Certainly it's possible. And, if you ask me, it's wise.

Director: Why is it wise?

Artist: Because there's nothing in this world we can be certain of except what we create.

Director: But what if we're not even certain of that? What if we have no idea what we create?

Artist: No idea? Then we're as lost as we can be.

~ Fit (Artist, Director, Heir, Sage)

Artist: There's no wisdom in consensus.

Sage: Oh, but of course there is!

Artist: How so?

Sage: It's simple. When our imperfect wisdoms come together, what is there but greater wisdom?

Director: We each hold a piece of the puzzle?

Sage: Yes, that puts it very well.

Artist: But then that means if even one piece is missing the puzzle is incomplete, is less than wisdom.

Sage: Well, yes, that's true. But isn't that all the more reason to search out all of the pieces?

Heir: But then we can never be wise on our own?

Sage: Of course we can. But there's wise, and then there's wise. Individual wisdom, greater wisdom.

Director: Which of those two would you prefer to have?

Sage: I'd like to have them both, Director. I'd like my individual wisdom to fit into something greater, something that makes it whole.

Artist: You can't be whole on your own?

Sage: What puzzle piece can?

Heir: But what if we urgently seek wholeness by trying to fit into some puzzle — and we force ourselves into someplace bad?

Sage: The wrong puzzle or the wrong place in the right puzzle? Either way, that's very unfortunate, and happens all the time. You just have to keep on trying, Heir.

Heir: But what if, try as I might, I just can't find my fit?

Sage: Then you should be open to your fit finding you.

~ Knowledge (Director, Heir)

Heir: Director, what do you think is the greatest component of wisdom?

Director: Well, I'm inclined to say it's knowledge.

Heir: Why are you only inclined?

Director: Because I'm simplifying things. Knowledge isn't enough. You have to know what to do with your knowledge.

Heir: But that's just another form of knowledge.

Director: Yes, you need knowledge about knowledge.

Heir: Then why don't you need knowledge about knowledge about knowledge?

Director: Ah, you understand the problem.

Heir: That's all you're going to say?

Director: What can I say?

Heir: You can say that something else is the greatest component of wisdom.

Director: Oh? What?

Heir: I don't know.

Director: Why yes, I think you're right.

Heir: What do you mean?

Director: The most important part of wisdom is knowing what you don't know.

Heir: But what if you don't know anything? Can you truly be wise?

Director: Heir, who knows nothing, absolutely nothing?

Heir: No one, I suppose.

Director: Yes. So the wise know what they don't know, and know what they do know.

Heir: But what do you think they know?

Director: If I knew that, I'd be wise.

~ Judgment (Artist, Sage)

Artist: Sage, do the wise pass judgment?

Sage: What do you mean?

Artist: You know. Do they judge people?

Sage: Yes and no.

Artist: How so?

Sage: Have you ever heard of 'judge' in the following sense? 'How high do you judge that tower to be?'

Artist: Yes.

Sage: Well, that's the sense in which you judge people. You form an estimate.

Artist: An estimate of what?

Sage: Them.

Artist: How tall they are?

Sage: In a sense.

Artist: Ha! Tell me about this sense.

Sage: Have you heard people talk about standing up straight and tall, not literally, but in a moral sense?

Artist: Yes, of course.

Sage: That's the sense I mean.

Artist: Okay. But you first said 'yes and no' when it comes to judging people. You've explained your yes. Now what about your no?

Sage: The wise don't often condemn others.

Artist: Why not? I condemn others all the time.

Sage: Yes, but do you know why these others are the way they are? The wise know when they don't know this. And they refuse to blame until they do.

~ Intelligence (Director, Sage)

Director: Tell me, Sage. Do you have to be intelligent in order to be wise?

Sage: Highly intelligent? No. Someone of average intelligence can be wise.

Director: What about someone of below average intelligence?

Sage: Wisdom doesn't depend on intelligence.

Director: But if not for intelligence, then how does someone become wise?

Sage: Well, of course some degree of intelligence is necessary. You have to be able to figure things out.

Director: Figure what things out?

Sage: Oh, Director. Don't tease. We all know there are things to figure out.

Director: Do you mean like the crossword puzzle in the newspaper?

Sage: No, of course not.

Director: Then what kind of things?

Sage: People.

Director: We figure people out like a puzzle? But what happens if we can't figure certain people out?

Sage: Then we're not wise.

Director: So in order to be wise, we have to figure everyone out?

Sage: Let's say there are degrees of wisdom.

Director: Hmm. But can we skip ahead? Can we figure out the hardest people first, before the easiest?

Sage: If you figure the hardest out first, can they really be that hard to you?

Director: So what sort of person is hard to understand?

Sage: Someone who's unlike — the low for the high, and the high for the low.

Director: But isn't knowledge of self hardest to achieve? And if self... then like?

~ Sense (Artist, Heir, Sage)

Artist: No, I'm not talking about having common sense. I'm talking about simply having sense. That's what makes you wise.

Heir: But why doesn't common sense make you wise?

Sage: Let me guess. It's because common sense is available to everyone, while sense, in your sense, belongs only to few.

Artist: Yes, Sage. That's exactly why.

Heir: You don't think everyone has the potential to be wise?

Artist: No, I don't.

Heir: I beg to differ.

Artist: Oh? Why?

Heir: Well, only if you have sense can you make sense, right?

Artist: I agree.

Heir: So if you make sense aren't you wise?

Artist: You make it sound so easy, Heir. But not everyone makes, or can make, sense.

Sage: What do we mean by 'making sense'?

Artist: Standing up under scrutiny. In other words, if we examine everything you say, it has to all add up without contradiction. That means you have sense. That means you're wise.

Sage: Yes, but what if those who aren't yet wise just need some help?

Artist: And let me guess. That's the help you try to give your advisees. Help to make them make good sense.

Sage: I help them make sense of their lives, and then I help them make good sense.

Artist: Then let me guess further. You yourself have to make good sense when you help them make their sense — or the whole effort is for naught.

Sage: Yes. And that's why, based on my success, I'm not afraid to say — I'm wise.

~ Shrewdness (Artist, Heir)

Artist: That Sage is a shrewd one.

Heir: Why do you say that?

Artist: Anyone who can lay claim to being wise is shrewd, in my opinion.

Heir: Yes, but I don't know if you think shrewdness is good or bad.

Artist: Heir! How can shrewdness not be good?

Heir: I'm thinking about the old meaning of the word 'shrewd'.

Artist: Oh? What's the meaning?

Heir: Mischievous or malicious.

Artist: You think Sage is mischievous or malicious?

Heir: No. Do you?

Artist: Of course not! Sage seems to me to be mostly earnest and well intentioned. He's sort of like you in that way.

Heir: Do you think I'm shrewd?

Artist: Ha! Maybe in the good sense of the word.

Heir: Good and shrewd like Sage? But why do I get the sense you're being ironic when you say that?

Artist: Ironic? How so? What do you think irony is?

Heir: Director once told me. He said irony is the dissembling of your superiority.

Artist: Director told you that? Well, then you must think I think I'm somehow superior when I praise you, ironically, for being shrewd! Perhaps I'm more shrewd than you!

Heir: Maybe in the old sense.

Artist: Which sense of the old sense? Mischievous or malicious?

Heir: Oh, definitely not malicious.

Artist: So, you think I'm superior in mischief? Well, why would I argue with that?

~ Interlude (Director, Heir)

Director: The guests are really starting to arrive.

Heir: Yes, and it's not too far past the time on the invitations. I'm glad you showed up right on time.

Director: Oh, I didn't want to miss a thing. But really, Heir. To start a lavish party at noon and carry it into breakfast on the following day?

Heir: What's wrong with that?

Director: Aren't you spending a small fortune?

Heir: True, but I graduate from graduate school only once. Isn't that worth spending something on?

Director: Maybe. But that's not all you're spending it on. What does Sage think?

Heir: It was Sage's idea!

Director: What? Why did he recommend this?

Heir: He said I needed to feel myself at the center of things right from the start.

Director: Does he think so poorly of you?

Heir: What do you mean?

Director: You, Heir, even without this party, would find yourself in the center of things.

Heir: And why do you think that is?

Director: Ah, you're fishing for praise. Well, I'll tell you what you already know. You're magnificently rich, strikingly handsome, highly intelligent, and of mostly good character. What more do you need?

Heir: I need this party.

Director: And that's why I'm here.

Heir: Oh? It's not because you simply enjoy being at big events?

Director: No, Heir, it's because it's your big event. Your launch into politics. And I think that's bigger than the people here might know.

~ Great Days (Artist, Sage)

Artist: Look at them with their champagne flutes. It's a thirsty crowd out there.

Sage: I'm so happy for Heir.

Artist: Why?

Sage: Because he's always wanted a party like this.

Artist: And what about me? Are you happy for me?

Sage: Why would I be?

Artist: Because I've always wanted to walk around sipping champagne! But what about you?

Sage: Am I so happy for me?

Artist: Yes. Is this something you've always wanted to do?

Sage: To support a friend on his great day? Yes, of course.

Artist: But why do you say it's a great day?

Sage: What greater than having all of your many friends come out to celebrate with you?

Artist: I've had greater days all by myself. Have you?

Sage: Well, my greatest days come in my office when I'm giving advice.

Artist: So not all by yourself.

Sage: No. But do you think that's somehow not as good as your greater days?

Artist: Oh, I don't mean to compare. Your way is your way and mine is mine. But....

Sage: But what?

Artist: My way will always be sounder than yours.

Sage: How so?

Artist: I depend on one thing — my art — while you depend on two — your art and your advisee. There's simply less to go wrong.

~ Sharing (Artist, Heir, Sage)

Heir: It's going so well, don't you think?

Sage: Absolutely. It's a wonderful party — and it's only getting started.

Heir: How are you doing, Artist?

Artist: Well, I'm finding it very hard.

Heir: Hard? Oh no! What's wrong?

Artist: I have to share all this fine food and wine — when I'd rather have it all to myself!

Heir: No you wouldn't. I know you like to share.

Artist: How do you know that?

Heir: Because you love sharing your work.

Artist: But, really, I only love to share with those who can appreciate my work.

Heir: And you don't think these people appreciate the food and wine?

Artist: I don't know, Heir. They don't seem to be paying much attention as they guzzle and munch.

Sage: But that's a good sign, Artist.

Artist: How so?

Sage: They're too busy sharing themselves to pay much attention to what's being served.

Artist: But what are they truly sharing, O Wise One? You can't just say 'themselves'.

Sage: They're sharing their souls.

Artist: In the things they say?

Sage: Yes. And what greater sharing can there be?

Artist: What greater? Ha! An honest sharing of souls.

Heir: But, Artist, what's more honest than the sharing that comes through wine? I think we'd better get back out there and have some more champagne!

~ Truth (Director, Heir)

Director: Do you believe people tell the truth when they're drunk?

Heir: Yes and no, Director.

Director: How so?

Heir: Does truth come out? Of course. But I think falsehood can, as well.

Director: How does falsehood come out?

Heir: When people spill certain truths, they sometimes realize what they've done, regret it, and backtrack to cover their trail with lies.

Director: Even while they're drunk? Then you can't believe everything a drunkard says.

Heir: No, of course not.

Director: But is there a way of sifting truth from lies?

Heir: Just keep your eye out for a backtrack.

Director: You can tell when people go back?

Heir: Almost always, yes.

Director: And everything before that is truth?

Heir: It is.

Director: I don't know if that's a wise assumption.

Heir: Why not?

Director: Because what if the drunkard spills what he or she thinks is truth, but it's not?

Heir: You mean drunks can be honest but not necessarily truthful?

Director: Yes, and that's often the way of it. No?

Heir: Then what's the use of hunting truth from drunks?

Director: Not much, Heir — unless you simply want to know the truth about what they think.

~ Melancholy (Director, Sage)

Sage: I've always found it to be somewhat melancholy behind the scenes.

Director: But, Sage, this is a cheery kitchen. Everything is bright and new and well ordered.

Sage: Yes, of course. But if that's enough to cheer you up, then I'd say there's something wrong with you.

Director: But I feel cheered in being here. So what's wrong with me?

Sage: Oh, Director. I wasn't talking about you.

Director: You were talking about yourself?

Sage: Yes, I suppose I was. I won't allow myself to be cheered by such superficial things.

Director: Then what cheers you, Sage?

Sage: My work.

Director: Getting down into the depths of your advisees' troubles?

Sage: Yes, getting down into the depths of melancholy and...

Director: ...finding your way out?

Sage: Yes.

Director: When you find your way out of the depths, don't you arrive at the surface?

Sage: Well, that's true.

Director: And the surface is superficial?

Sage: I don't know if I'd put it that way.

Director: Hmm. You know, Heir seems to appreciate the superficial. I've heard him speak of this kitchen several times in praise.

Sage: Yes, but Heir has a deeper side, too. I'd like to help bring that out.

Director: Bring his depths to the surface? I only hope that doesn't ruin his good cheer.

- Joy (Heir, Sage)

Sage: It occurs to me, Heir, that we've hardly spent enough time talking about joy.

Heir: Well, this is a fine time to speak of it!

Sage: Yes. But do you say that because you feel joy here and now?

Heir: Of course! The party is off to such a good start.

Sage: But is it true joy you feel?

Heir: What else could it be?

Sage: Mere excitement.

Heir: If this is what excitement feels like — I like it!

Sage: Yes, but do you remember what we said in your last session?

Heir: The ends don't have to justify the means?

Sage: No, not that.

Heir: That we should be wary of excitement?

Sage: Yes. And do you remember why?

Heir: Excitement can corrupt our judgment.

Sage: And?

Heir: And that's not very wise. So what does this have to do with joy?

Sage: When you feel excitement, ask yourself how it could be joy.

Heir: It could be joy if I keep my judgment intact?

Sage: And how do you do that?

Heir: By seeking something deeper than the froth of excitement.

Sage: Something like what we have in our talks?

Heir: Yes, Sage. But I think there can be joy in the froth of things, too. So let's get back out there and enjoy. And if my judgment seems off, I'll count on you to let me know.

~ Happiness (Director, Artist)

Artist: Heir sure looks happy.

Director: Yes, he does.

Artist: And I'm glad Sage is over there sulking and leaving him alone.

Director: Oh?

Artist: Sage is like a black cloud following him around.

Director: Why do you say that?

Artist: Because he's in love with him!

Director: But it's odd, no? It usually works the other way.

Artist: You mean the advisee falls in love with the advisor?

Director: Isn't that often how it goes?

Artist: Not in this case, obviously.

Director: Do you think Sage is bad for Heir?

Artist: No, not necessarily. He is wise, after all.

Director: I don't think Sage is all bad. And he might have a good influence on Heir.

Artist: How so?

Director: He'll make Heir realize that just because someone is in love with you, that doesn't mean they'll make you happy.

Artist: Ha! Yes, a very good lesson to learn — but one I think Heir already knows. But what will make him happy?

Director: He's the only one who can say. But judging from the looks of him at this party, I think he's found at least one thing that makes him feel good.

Artist: Yes, yes. But everyone loves to play the host.

Director: Everyone? Do you?

Artist: Well, no. And neither do you.

~ Leadership (Artist, Director, Heir, Sage)

Director: Heir, I can see you have the makings of a real leader.

Heir: How so, Director?

Director: Everywhere you go today, a small crowd gathers around you.

Heir: Oh, they're just being polite to the host.

Sage: No, I think Director is right. There's something more to it.

Artist: What exactly do you think it is, Sage?

Sage: Heir has charisma.

Artist: Charisma? What on earth is that?

Sage: You know, Artist. Charisma results in what Director sees.

Artist: So you're saying Heir is attractive?

Sage: It's something more than being attractive.

Director: It's being attractive in a larger sense, in a compelling sense?

Sage: Yes, exactly.

Heir: Well, thank you all for finding me to be so attractive! But it takes more to lead.

Artist: I'll say it does. And I'm not so sure you have it.

Director: Why so harsh, Artist?

Artist: He needs to know the truth.

Director: But I think he has great potential to lead.

Sage: And so do I.

Artist: So tell us, Sage, what does that potential involve?

Sage: Wisdom.

Artist: And Heir is wise? Ha! I don't think even he would agree with you on that.

Sage: But when it comes to leading, his agreement isn't what counts.

- Neither (Artist, Heir)

Heir: Artist, I genuinely want to know — why do you doubt I have what it takes to lead?

Artist: Do you think you have what it takes to lead?

Heir: Yes, but I want to know why you think I don't.

Artist: Don't you think you lack wisdom?

Heir: I do. But I'm young. And I can learn.

Artist: Leaders have to learn quicker than most.

Heir: Then teach me.

Artist: I can't teach you wisdom, Heir. Wisdom is something I lack.

Heir: Of course. And I suppose Director lacks wisdom, too. Only Sage has wisdom.

Artist: Maybe you should become a follower of Sage.

Heir: Sarcasm aside, do you think followers can ever grow wise?

Artist: No, not if all you are is a follower.

Heir: You have to lead to be wise?

Artist: Do you think leading and following is all there is?

Heir: What else is there?

Artist: Doing neither.

Heir: Like you?

Artist: Yes, like me.

Heir: But you're not wise.

Artist: I'm wise enough not to say I am.

Heir: Then you're a hypocrite? You're wise but say you're not?

Artist: Ha! That's the opposite of hypocrisy. But now you're showing the bud of wisdom.

Heir: By challenging you? Then being wise is easier than I thought.

~ Patience (Artist, Heir, Sage)

Sage: The guests are pouring in.

Heir: Yes, and I'm grateful I get to take a breather back here with you!

Artist: I don't know how you have the patience to deal with all those people.

Heir: Why do you say that?

Artist: Doesn't it get tiresome?

Heir: Why, no! I find it enlivening.

Sage: A sign of a good leader.

Artist: Yes, sure. But I still think Heir is exercising patience.

Sage: Patience is another sign of a good leader.

Artist: Is it a sign of wisdom?

Sage: It is.

Artist: Is being enlivened by people a sign of wisdom?

Sage: Well, not necessarily.

Artist: So only part of what Heir is showing today smacks of wisdom?

Heir: There's more to leadership than wisdom, Artist.

Artist: Oh, I couldn't agree with you more. But as far as wisdom goes, is patience always something a leader needs?

Heir: Yes, but not if you take it too far.

Artist: Then tell me. How far should your patience go?

Heir: Only as far as the bounds of reason.

Artist: But how do you know where those bounds lie?

Heir: If I no longer feel enlivened, I know I've crossed the line.

Artist: Then what a lively leader you'll be!

- Philosophy (Director, Sage)

Director: Sage, I'm glad we've got a moment alone.

Sage: Oh? Why, Director?

Director: I wanted to ask you something about philosophy.

Sage: What do you want to know?

Director: Do you know what philosophy is?

Sage: It's the love of wisdom.

Director: Yes. But now here's what I want to know. You're wise, right?

Sage: I don't make overly much of the fact, but yes.

Director: So do you have philosophers flocking around you?

Sage: Ha, ha. No, Director. I don't.

Director: Why do you think that is?

Sage: Maybe it's because philosophers love wisdom but not the wise.

Director: What's this? But where would they get wisdom if not from the wise?

Sage: From books, for one, in an indirect way.

Director: For one, certainly. But what about wisdom repeated by others at second hand?

Sage: I suppose that's where philosophers find much of their wisdom.

Director: Hmm. Yes. But tell me. How can a philosopher recognize this wisdom as wisdom if the wise one who coined it isn't there?

Sage: It's as it is with books. The author's not there, but the wisdom speaks.

Director: Oh, but the author is certainly there — sometimes more so than in person.

Sage: Well, maybe that's how it is with the wise and those who repeat their wisdom.

Director: Are you saying those who repeat the wisdom are like books in which the wise ones write? But if that were so, wouldn't a repeater always repeat exactly what the wise one said, in the same context in which it was said? But that's not how it goes.

- Recognition (Artist, Director, Heir)

Artist: But is it enough to be wise?

Director: What do you mean?

Heir: Yes, what are you saying, Artist?

Artist: I'm asking this: Would you want to be wise if it involved no one ever recognizing you as wise?

Director: No one? Ever? That seems a little hard. Don't we all need a little recognition now and then?

Heir: I think Artist is asking a good question. And for me the answer is, yes, it wouldn't matter if I'm never recognized as wise.

Director: But if you still have thoughts of being a leader, wouldn't others have to recognize your wisdom?

Heir: I would distinguish between being recognized as wise and being recognized as great.

Artist: Ha! You see, Director? He's showing more signs of wisdom all the time.

Director: But if you're not a wise leader, what kind of leader are you? You say 'great' — but what constitutes greatness?

Heir: Many things. Courage. Resolve. Honesty. Justice. Skill. Persuasiveness. Moderation. And many more!

Director: Then what's left for wisdom?

Heir: Knowing how to use all those things I just listed. Those are the things people see. Wisdom is something you have inside.

Director: And you think you could live your whole life without being acknowledged as wise?

Heir: If that's the choice? Being known as great without being known as wise? Yes!

Artist: So long as you knew you had the underlying wisdom to make yourself great?

Heir: So long as I knew. And maybe if you knew, too — but kept your mouths shut.

~ Acknowledgement (Artist, Director)

Artist: You truly think he has that much potential to lead?

Director: I do.

Artist: But I don't think he was being serious.

Director: Why not?

Artist: You think he'd worry that you and I would expose his wisdom?

Director: How could he not?

Artist: But why would that be a problem?

Director: Great leaders keep their own counsel. Don't you agree?

Artist: No. A great leader takes counsel from many.

Director: Yes, of course. But then when it comes time to weigh reasons and decide?

Artist: Well, yes. I suppose you have a point.

Director: And once Heir weighs and decides, should he come running to us to tell us everything he thinks, to spill his wisdom, his guts?

Artist: No, not at all. He must, in his heart of hearts, be his own man.

Director: So if we're able to guess the secret thoughts that went into his plans, would we be friends to him to proclaim these thoughts to others?

Artist: Of course not.

Director: Then if he proves to be a great leader, we can't acknowledge his wisdom, the real reason for his success.

Artist: I guess we can't.

Director: Can you live with that?

Artist: No.

Director: Then what will you do?

Artist: Bury myself in my work, and force myself to have nothing to say.

~ Osmosis (Artist, Heir)

Artist: Why are you here all alone in the library? What's the matter? Not feeling very energized by your guests?

Heir: I was hoping I might pick up some wisdom by osmosis.

Artist: Ha! Well, your friend Sage isn't here. And the only things you might pick up from me are things you'd want to get rid of!

Heir: I know you don't really believe that.

Artist: What makes you say so?

Heir: I think you have a wisdom of your own.

Artist: My own special wisdom? A wisdom for half-wit artists?

Heir: Do you have any idea what I've learned from your works?

Artist: That's a hard question for an artist to answer. I like to think I know what's in my works. But then every so often someone comes up and tells me what they found in them, and I'm shocked! I had no idea any of those things were even there.

Heir: Well, then we'll have to sit down some time and review what I think I've learned.

Artist: Yes, but let's do it over drinks. I don't think I could stand a conversation like that sober.

Heir: What do you think of Sage?

Artist: I think you have a high opinion of him. So I'll say he seems decent enough to me.

Heir: Do you think he's wise?

Artist: He certainly has that reputation. And he's wise enough to have to do with you. So there's some wisdom in there.

Heir: I suspect Director doesn't like him very much.

Artist: Oh, I think Director likes him more than I do.

Heir: Which doesn't say much?

Artist: Which says enough.

~ Teaching (Artist, Director, Heir, Sage)

Sage: The truly wise teach.

Artist: Why?

Sage: When you're overflowing with something, you want to share. And with the works of yours I've seen, I think you do just that.

Heir: I agree, Sage. And I think Director teaches, too.

Director: What do I teach?

Heir: Philosophy!

Director: But what does that mean?

Heir: You teach people how to think.

Director: How to think? Is that like teaching people how to drive? Once they know how, they go wherever they like?

Sage: I think that's an excellent point. You teach people independence.

Director: Is that what you teach?

Sage: Yes.

Director: So, essentially, you and I teach just the same thing? But don't you often suggest to people where to go?

Sage: Well, yes. Don't you?

Director: Not really. Heir, have I ever suggested to you where to go or what to do?

Heir: You've questioned why I want to go where I want to go and do what I want to do. And you've pointed out problems in my thinking. But no, you've never suggested anything like that.

Sage: Why not, Director?

Director: Because I don't know what's best for anyone but me — and not even always that. Do you?

Sage: For me? Yes, of course. And I'm not afraid to admit — I often know for others, too.

- Experience (Artist, Director, Heir, Sage)

Artist: But how do you know what's best for others?

Sage: I consider my own life experience and seek parallels in those I advise.

Artist: And you assume if there's a parallel, what's good for you is good for them?

Sage: In a general sense? Yes.

Artist: Ha! Director, is what's good for you good for others?

Director: Philosophy? Yes, of course. But I think there's an important difference between philosophy and Sage's psychology.

Heir: Let me guess. Philosophy never treats A and B as the same.

Artist: Sage, do you ever treat A and B as the same?

Sage: I do in this sense. If I experience A, and you experience B, my psychology says our experiences can be essentially the same.

Artist: They can? And that's true even if you experience ABC and I experience XYZ?

Sage: Yes. But I need to clarify something. What counts is how we feel about the experience, not what the experience actually is.

Artist: Then if I feel anger about XYZ, and you feel delight, there's no parallel?

Sage: As far as that particular experience is concerned? True.

Artist: So you wouldn't know what's best for me.

Sage: Well, not necessarily. You might have felt delight at another time in your life. We'd have a parallel in that. In that we could relate.

Artist: And the more and various things we feel, the greater the chance we'll find something in common?

Sage: Yes.

Director: I think Sage has faith in what he'd call the common experience of humanity.

Sage: I do. But this faith can be hard, since the wise experience certain things sooner than their peers. And then they have to wait.

~ Relating (Artist, Director, Heir, Sage)

Artist: But if our common experience came at the same time, we could all easily relate?

Sage: Certainly.

Artist: But when we relate, we relate with what's the same in us. So we'd be the same?

Sage: Essentially the same, as far as we relate — yes.

Artist: And if we relate a very great deal, there'd be little individuality?

Heir: No, Artist. Sage thinks we're all individuals, but closer to the surface.

Artist: Ha! Is that what you're saying, Sage?

Sage: Yes.

Artist: And what's on the surface? The way we look? The clothes we wear? What?

Sage: The things we bring up from our depths.

Director: But aren't the depths, our essence, where you think we're all the same?

Sage: Yes, Director. But we all bring up different things.

Director: Well, Artist doesn't look pleased. But tell us, Sage. Is passion important?

Sage: Of course.

Director: And do you think we all feel the same passions, if not at the same time, then at some point in our lives?

Sage: Mostly.

Artist: Ridiculous! You really think most of us feel the great passions in life?

Heir: If not, how would we know?

Artist: If so, how would we know?

Sage: We'd know, for instance, through what we experience in great art.

Heir: Because those who appreciate great art relate to the passions the artist conveys?

Sage: Yes. And if we relate, doesn't that mean we've felt? So, Artist, what do you say?

~ Essence (Artist, Director, Heir, Sage)

Sage: The wise understand the urge to explain.

Director: What do they understand about it?

Sage: That explanation leads us back to our common humanity.

Artist: But not all of us have the urge to explain.

Sage: That's because some of us are blocked.

Artist: Blocked? You interpret a noble reserve as a failing?

Sage: You interpret a failing as a noble reserve.

Artist: So tell us. What good comes of this common humanity of yours?

Sage: The same good that comes of knowing the truth.

Artist: The truth that we're all essentially the same?

Sage: Yes.

Heir: Artist, you don't think we are?

Artist: No, Heir, I don't.

Director: What proof do you have?

Artist: Look at it this way. Two houses might be made with bricks. The bricks are essentially the same. But one house is beautiful and the other is not. Are the houses the same because they're both made with bricks?

Heir: I think that's an excellent point. Sage, what do you think?

Sage: I think that misses the point.

Artist: And what's the point?

Sage: That we should explain why we see one house as beautiful and the other as not.

Director: And once we explain?

Sage: We'll know how to fix the ugly one up.

~ Habit (Artist, Director, Heir, Sage)

Sage: Of course the wise form habits.

Heir: What kind of habits do they form?

Sage: They try to form good ones.

Artist: But that's not all the habits they form.

Sage: What do you mean?

Artist: They form neutral habits.

Heir: What's a neutral habit?

Artist: Well, Heir, I see you're in the habit of swirling your wine. Would you say that's a good habit?

Heir: No, I wouldn't say it is.

Artist: Is it a bad habit?

Heir: No, it's not. So you've made your point. A neutral habit. But how do we know when something is a good habit, or a bad habit for that matter?

Sage: What do you mean? It's obvious!

Director: It doesn't seem obvious to him. Maybe he needs a standard by which to judge.

Heir: Yes, I think that's an excellent idea! A standard.

Sage: What would your standard be?

Heir: For now? Getting elected.

Artist: Ha! You'd judge all of your habits based on that? Every single one?

Heir: Yes, even the swirl of my wine. That little habit, as I use it, shows confidence and ease — things that will help me win.

Sage: So you're talking about having a true singleness of purpose?

Heir: I am. And now that we're clear about my intent, I trust no one will object if I change a few habits to bring them into line.

~ Perception (Artist, Director, Heir, Sage)

Sage: If you perceive something, that's your reality.

Artist: And if you perceive something as true that's not, what's your reality?

Sage: It depends on how many others think it's true.

Heir: You really can't mean that, Sage.

Sage: Of course I can. And that's how you must look at it, too — if you intend to lead.

Heir: But I want to be the kind of leader who tells people the truth!

Sage: The truth is that they think their perception is reality — and, in a sense, it is. So you must recognize this truth.

Director: Because a leader deals in opinions?

Sage: Yes, Director.

Director: But surely he or she should know the truth about those opinions.

Sage: That's best, yes.

Heir: So I'm to be wise to people's opinions but hide my wisdom?

Sage: Except for when opportunity arises.

Heir: Such as now, among my intimate friends?

Sage: As you say.

Heir: And then I'm to be a hypocrite or worse? Saying one thing to you and another to them? No. I think it's best when I lead to say the same thing to all.

Sage: Then, if you're to lead, you must cloak your wisdom from all.

Heir: And if I don't lead?

Sage: But why wouldn't you lead?

Heir: Maybe because I don't want to hide what I know.

Artist: Oh, all of us to one degree or another hide what we know. So stop worrying and prepare yourself to lead.

~ Action (Artist, Director, Heir, Sage)

Director: Sage, what do you do, what's your 'action', or 'act', for those you advise?

Sage: I speak my wisdom, my truth.

Director: Only to those you advise?

Sage: Well, of course not only. But for the most part? Yes.

Director: And you only advise one at a time, in private?

Sage: That's right.

Artist: Ha!

Sage: What is it now?

Artist: It just occurred to me. Who's to say whether you actually speak the same wisdom, or truth as you call it, all the time, to each advisee?

Sage: If I didn't, word might get out and ruin my reputation.

Artist: So your 'act' is the building of your reputation?

Sage: No, my act is helping others. And I happen to have a reputation for that.

Artist: Well, my act is my craft. But I don't just 'happen' to have a reputation for that.

Heir: My act is to lead. And I'll have a deliberate reputation for that. And you, Director?

Director: My act is to philosophize.

Sage: And what does that entail?

Director: Helping myself and others know what we can through discussion.

Sage: And your reputation?

Artist: I'll tell you. It depends who you ask. And I hope his reputation with you, Sage, will be that he helps people know that they don't know!

Director: That may be how it turns out. But, Sage, I'm hoping you can help me know, know what wisdom is. You see, I'm very selfish. I want to know — for me. If we can know together, you and I, that's wonderful. But I'm not afraid to know on my own.

- Self-Control (Heir, Sage)

Sage: I don't quite know what to make of Director.

Heir: Why do you say that?

Sage: Why do you think he was talking about not being afraid to know on his own?

Heir: I don't know. Why do you think he was?

Sage: He was hinting I'm afraid of being wise on my own.

Heir: No, I don't think he was hinting that. But are you?

Sage: It's not a matter of being afraid. It's a matter of wanting to share.

Heir: So you don't want to be wise on your own?

Sage: I'd rather not.

Heir: I think keeping your wisdom to yourself would take a great deal of self-control.

Sage: Yes, but self-control can be misguided. What good is holding back the flood if you're holding back something good?

Heir: But isn't wisdom always good, no matter if it's held back?

Sage: Well, we did speak of leaders cloaking their wisdom from all.

Heir: And that doesn't make their wisdom any less good. Wisdom is good no matter what. Why, even in silent snakes!

Sage: Oh, Heir, people do say serpents are wise. But that doesn't mean it's true.

Heir: You don't think serpents are wise?

Sage: I don't know. But if they are, I know they don't always exercise self-control.

Heir: How do you know that?

Sage: Because they have a reputation for being wise! And how do you think they got that reputation? By keeping their wisdom all to themselves?

Heir: Some say holding your tongue is the surest sign of wisdom.

Sage: Yes, but if you hold it too long, what builds up — but one great big hiss?

~ Principles (Artist, Director, Heir)

Director: Oh, Heir. Artist and I were just discussing something and we wonder what you think.

Heir: What were you discussing?

Director: Whether wisdom involves having certain principles.

Heir: And what did you two say?

Artist: I said wisdom involves having no principles at all.

Heir: Why did you say that?

Artist: Why do you think I said it? Because Director said, in his experience, wisdom involves principles.

Heir: And you just wanted to contradict?

Artist: More or less? Yes! But it's really what I think. So what do you think?

Heir: I think wisdom definitely involves principles.

Artist: Yes, but what do you mean by 'involves'? Should we take it in the old sense, as in 'entangles'?

Heir: What? No. I mean, for you to be wise, you must have principles.

Director: What principles must you have?

Heir: For instance? Do you remember all the things I listed before, things a great leader needs? Courage and so on? Principles like that.

Artist: But those aren't principles. Those are qualities, traits.

Heir: Yes, but every one of those qualities is backed by at least one principle.

Director: Can they all be backed by the same principle?

Heir: What principle would that be?

Artist: Ha! I'll tell you what principle that would be, the only one I'd allow. The principle of self-interest, my friend. The principle of need.

~ Morals (Artist, Heir, Sage)

Artist: Tell us, Sage. What does wisdom make of morals?

Sage: Make of morals? It makes much.

Artist: Oh, but you have to say more than that. What does it take to make much of morals?

Sage: It takes seeing their true worth.

Artist: Which is much?

Sage: Which is very much.

Artist: Name a moral that's worth very much.

Sage: Being kind to others.

Artist: Is it always wise to be kind to others?

Sage: For any one of us in our private lives? Always.

Heir: Even if it's a vile person?

Sage: Even so, Heir.

Artist: Ha! Why would you be kind to the vile?

Sage: Because it's likely no one else is.

Heir: I think he has a point, Artist.

Artist: But what's the point? To do the opposite of what everyone else does? So that if everyone tells the truth, we should lie? Is that wisdom?

Sage: You know it's not.

Artist: Do I? I don't know. What's wise if everyone is wise in the same way?

Heir: You mean, then what's so special about being wise?

Artist: Yes.

Sage: But you assume the wise want to be special. Not so! The wise wish they weren't so special. They wish everyone were wise like them — so they'd be less alone.

~ Discernment (Director, Heir)

Director: I can hardly believe it. More and more people arriving all the time.

Heir: And they'll keep coming all day and all through the night.

Director: With so many guests, how do you discern your true friends, Heir?

Heir: Every guest is a friend, and every friend is a true friend, Director.

Director: Ah, some wisdom from Sage?

Heir: Sage does say every friend should be treated as a true friend.

Director: But you have a great many friends. Do you really have time to treat them all as your true friends?

Heir: I simply have to ration my time. And they understand.

Director: Then I'm flattered you keep coming back to speak with me. But maybe I'm no true friend.

Heir: Why in the world would you say that?

Director: What is a true friend?

Heir: Someone you can count on.

Director: Count on to do what?

Heir: Be there for you and tell you the truth.

Director: And all of these many guests are here for you now. They really came through to attend this magnificent party. And I'm certain if they drink enough of your delicious wine, most of them will start spilling out their versions of the truth. And that's a true friend.

Heir: Ha, ha. I suppose you've caught me.

Director: In what?

Heir: The lie that every friend is a true friend. But it's a noble lie.

Director: A noble lie? It seems more like a vote-getting lie to me. And that, my friend, is a truth I offer you today.

~ Insight (Artist, Director)

Artist: I think Heir has many insights into human nature.

Director: So do I. But what will he do with them?

Artist: Advance a political career, what else?

Director: Is that the best use of his wisdom?

Artist: Well, you don't think he could be an artist, do you?

Director: He hasn't developed any artistic skills.

Artist: Do you think he could be a philosopher?

Director: Potentially? Yes. But he's not interested in that.

Artist: How about a business leader?

Director: As a stepping stone to politics, sure.

Artist: What do you think he sees in politics?

Director: I think he sees it as his highest calling.

Artist: Is he right?

Director: I'm afraid so.

Artist: Why are you afraid?

Director: Because he has the insights it will take to climb. But those very insights will torture him once he makes it to the top. I've told him this.

Artist: But why will his insights torture him?

Director: Because he'll see all that can be in stark contrast to all that is — and he'll want more and more power to make things as he would have them.

Artist: But politics is about necessity, not what you might like.

Director: True. But it's also about the possible. And if something is possible, it's necessary. No?

Artist: Maybe in some philosophical sense. And maybe as Heir sees it, too.

- Age (Director, Heir)

Director: I'm surprised, Heir.

Heir: Oh? Why?

Director: Look around. What do you see?

Heir: Guests. What do you see?

Director: I see a great mix of ages, from those as young as you to those older than me.

Heir: What's so surprising about that?

Director: Young people typically, and especially at parties, want to be surrounded by the young. Why do you think that is?

Heir: They think older people can't understand them and will put a damper on things.

Director: But you don't think that way. Why?

Heir: I understand older people. And so they can understand something of me.

Director: Understanding brings understanding, to some degree?

Heir: Of course.

Director: And understanding is never a damper?

Heir: No, never. Understanding enlivens.

Director: But how is it for your guests, aside from their relation to you? Do they understand one another across the ages?

Heir: For the most part? No.

Director: So you're the linchpin holding it all together, keeping it lively?

Heir: Well, it's my party. So don't you think that's an appropriate role for me to play?

Director: Yes, I do. But doesn't that mean you have a great responsibility?

Heir: Keeping a party lively is a great responsibility?

Director: Oh, yes. Certainly. Especially when the party is practice, practice for the party to be held one day for all of us — on the ship of state.

- Self-Knowledge (Artist, Director, Heir)

Artist: That saying 'know thyself' is mostly a distraction.

Heir: Why would you say that?

Artist: If you're so busy knowing yourself, what time do you have for anything else?

Heir: You don't think it's important to know yourself?

Artist: Yes, yes — it's important. But contrary to what many seem to think, you know yourself through what you do, not through endless contemplation.

Heir: But don't you have to contemplate what you've done?

Artist: Yes, but mostly you just do.

Heir: Director, do you go along with what Artist is saying?

Director: Well, what's he saying? That we must do, then think, and then move on?

Heir: Yes, I suppose.

Director: And that leaves us no time for contemplating our acts in the sense of chewing the cud?

Heir: But aren't there times when we have to ruminate, have to think deeply about what we've done?

Artist: Of course. But we must think things through, commit what we've learned to memory, and get back to work. We'll end up with more self-knowledge that way.

Heir: I think that makes sense. But do we ever share our self-knowledge?

Artist: Ha! Absolutely not.

Heir: Why?

Artist: Because whose business is that? It's ours alone.

Heir: And if we keep on hoarding self-knowledge, will we become wise?

Artist: Wise? Who cares? The use of self-knowledge is in what it can help us do. The use of wisdom — it's not always so clear.

~ Sincerity (Artist, Director, Heir)

Artist: Sincerity is overrated.

Heir: Ah, Artist. Count on you to say that.

Artist: But isn't it? Look at all these people here now. How many of them are being sincere?

Heir: It depends on who they're talking to.

Director: And if they were talking to you?

Heir: Some of them would be sincere.

Director: Only some?

Heir: Do you think everyone is sincere to everyone?

Director: No, Heir, I don't. But wouldn't you expect that those you invite to your home would be sincere to you?

Heir: Have you heard the saying, 'Keep your friends close and your enemies closer'?

Director: I have. But do you really have so many enemies, you who are just starting out on your path in life?

Heir: You'd be surprised.

Artist: How did you make so many enemies?

Heir: I inherited many of them.

Artist: So they're not really your enemies?

Heir: Oh, trust me — they are.

Director: But they don't speak sincerely to you?

Heir: Of course they don't.

Director: Why not? Why don't they say, 'Thank you for having me, but I am your enemy'?

Heir: Because enemies are rarely sincere!

Director: Then value those who are.

~ Integrity (Artist, Director, Heir)

Artist: So what does Sage say about integrity?

Heir: Why don't you ask him?

Artist: Because I want to know what he says to you.

Heir: Do you think he'd say different things to you and me?

Artist: He might.

Heir: Why?

Artist: He might think we have different levels of understanding. And a wise man always says different things to different people depending on their understanding. Isn't it true with you?

Heir: What makes you think it would be?

Artist: Look, when you speak to someone who's severely developmentally challenged, don't you say one thing? And when you speak to those not so challenged, don't you say another?

Heir: Well, yes.

Artist: It's the same with people in general. To those who understand we say one thing, and to those who don't we say another.

Heir: And what about integrity?

Artist: Integrity? Ha! That is integrity!

Heir: Oh, that can't be. Director, what do you think?

Director: I think Artist is getting at something important. But I wouldn't call what he's talking about integrity.

Heir: What would you call it?

Director: An ancient form of wisdom.

Heir: And how wise is it when people compare notes on the different things you've said?

Artist: Oh, it's still wise — so long as those with understanding know enough to deny the things they must.

~ Taste (Artist, Director, Heir)

Heir: There's no disputing tastes.

Artist: Oh, but there is! Haven't you heard that's what life is all about?

Heir: Life is a dispute about tastes?

Artist: Yes, yes — of course! Imagine what happens if you don't fight for your tastes.

Heir: I suppose you can't enjoy them.

Director: Yes. But tell us, Artist. Do the wise share tastes?

Artist: The truly wise? No. They have unique tastes they defend until the end.

Heir: But are there really so many tastes that the tastes of the wise can all be unique?

Artist: Well, of course there's some overlap. My tastes might incline to AEIOU and yours might incline to ABCDE. So we can share some tastes but still be unique.

Heir: Would you say the more overlap, the better friends the people in question can be?

Artist: Up to a point, yes. But they can't forget about what they don't share with the other.

Heir: What's wrong with forgetting about what you don't share?

Artist: You lose yourself.

Heir: Your tastes are yourself?

Artist: Actions, thoughts, and tastes. That's the whole of life.

Heir: So what if we share actions and thoughts but not our tastes?

Artist: Impossible. Tastes determine our actions and thoughts.

Heir: But you can't really believe that.

Artist: It's not a matter of belief.

Director: Artist, you don't think people think and act against their tastes all the time?

Artist: Of course they do. But then they're not really living their lives.

~ Divine (Artist, Director, Heir, Sage)

Artist: There's no such thing as divine wisdom.

Heir: All wisdom is human wisdom?

Artist: Yes, of course.

Sage: But surely we can be divinely inspired in our wisdom.

Artist: Surely? Ha! That inspiration is just a lie some people tell to get others to believe in their 'wisdom'.

Sage: Oh, I don't know. I think it's inexplicable in normal human terms how certain people come to be as wise as they are. Director, wouldn't you agree?

Director: I think it's hard to say how some people become so wise.

Artist: Hard but not impossible.

Heir: Can you say how they become so wise?

Artist: Find me someone who's all that wise and we'll see.

Sage: What about someone with a basic sort of wisdom?

Artist: Who, you?

Sage: Sure, why not? How did I become wise?

Artist: I'd have to get to know you better before I could say.

Sage: Why don't you come and see me sometime and we can talk? Then you can see whether you can figure me out, can determine if my inspiration is anything but divine.

Artist: Meanwhile you'll be trying to figure out me?

Sage: Only to see if my wisdom can be of use.

Artist: And if it is of use, you expect I'll come to see it as divinely inspired?

Sage: Why not?

Artist: Just because something is of use doesn't mean it derives from the divine.

Sage: True. It sometimes means it is, actually is — divine.

~ Concealed (Artist, Director, Heir, Sage)

Heir: It sometimes seems to me that wisdom, all wisdom, should be concealed.

Director: Hmm. Artist, what do you think?

Artist: I think it's true.

Sage: Well, then what else can I conclude but that you must think I'm foolish to go around admitting I'm wise?

Artist: Yes, Sage. We think you're foolish. Very foolish.

Sage: Tell me what exactly is foolish.

Artist: Wisdom is something you reveal only to your very close friends, if at all.

Sage: Why?

Artist: Because next to love, it's the most precious thing in the world.

Sage: Would you share your wisdom with those you love?

Heir: Yes, Sage, naturally we would.

Sage: And we love our friends?

Heir: Of course we do.

Sage: And we're all friends?

Artist: In varying degrees.

Sage: You mean me. I'm the varying degree.

Artist: Well, if you want me to be honest, then yes.

Sage: But what if I wish to share my wisdom with the three of you, on the basis of the strong friendship I think we'll develop?

Artist: Develop out of your wisdom? Ha! But maybe we should give it a try. So reveal your wisdom, Sage.

Sage: Ah, but if it were just that easy! Wisdom only becomes clear while discussing other things.

~ Convention (Artist, Director, Heir, Sage)

Director: We've all heard of conventional wisdom, right?

Heir: Yes, of course, Director.

Director: Well, would that ever have to be concealed?

Heir: No, not at all.

Director: What about unconventional wisdom? Would you ever have to conceal that?

Heir: It depends on how unconventional the wisdom is for the context you're in.

Director: Now, Sage, what sort of wisdom have you got?

Sage: I have both the conventional and the unconventional.

Director: Which do you share freely with one and all?

Sage: The conventional.

Director: And with whom would you share your unconventional wisdom?

Sage: With those I trust.

Director: Your friends?

Sage: Yes, with my friends.

Director: But tell us. What is it about your unconventional wisdom that requires such careful handling?

Sage: What is it about any unconventional wisdom? It's at odds with convention.

Director: And if at odds with that, at odds with those who support it? But who supports convention?

Sage: Most everyone.

Artist: Yes, Sage, and here's the question: Would you dare to stand openly opposed to convention, to most everyone, to nearly one and all — if that's how you can help your friends?

Sage: If that's truly how I can help my friends? Then I like to think I would.

~ Tradition (Artist, Director, Heir, Sage)

Artist: Is there wisdom in tradition?

Sage: According to many? Yes, of course.

Artist: But not in your opinion?

Sage: No. I believe there *can* be.

Artist: Can be? So when you advise people, does that mean sometimes your wisdom is traditional and sometimes it's something else? If so, what's that something else?

Sage: It's wisdom that's up-to-date.

Artist: Why not employ only the up-to-date?

Sage: Most people need tradition blended in.

Director: Why do you think that is?

Sage: Honestly? They're not strong enough to take the up-to-date straight.

Heir: What's so hard about that?

Sage: You deal directly with existing circumstances.

Heir: And the traditional doesn't?

Sage: The traditional always touches only in part on what's currently going on.

Heir: Even in a very traditional society?

Sage: Well, traditions have differing degrees of relevance, of course.

Director: So you have to judge the society before you give advice?

Sage: True.

Director: And you have to judge the individual in that society?

Sage: Yes.

Artist: That's a lot of judgment, Sage.

Sage: That's what it takes to be wise.

~ Originality (Artist, Director, Heir, Sage)

Artist: The untraditional, the unconventional — doesn't it all come down to being original?

Sage: Yes.

Heir: And can't everyone be original, if they really try?

Sage: Ah, Heir. You have to be strong, very strong to be completely original.

Heir: But who is ever completely original? In fact, I think the most original often have a great deal of the traditional and the conventional behind them.

Director: How so?

Heir: Sage said most people need tradition blended in. True. But what he should have said is that even the strongest do. And it holds for convention, too.

Artist: How?

Heir: I'll give you an example. Let's say there are ten things you can do. And you want one of them to be original, wildly original. You'll be better supported in your attempt if you have five traditional and four conventional things, for instance, to back you. Don't you agree?

Director: That certainly sounds plausible. But what if you succeed in your wild attempt?

Heir: Your original thing might well become convention, and even tradition, over a long enough stretch of time.

Director: Is that the goal, then? To become convention, to become tradition?

Heir: Do you see anything wrong with that?

Director: I have to say no. But what's the end? Why take the trouble to do this?

Heir: For the sake of originality!

Director: Don't you mean for the sake of fame?

Heir: Well, there's that.

Director: Do you see anything wrong with fame?

Heir: Not if it's deserved. Not if it's based on something original — and bold.

~ Epigones (Artist, Director, Heir, Sage)

Artist: Things tend to degenerate.

Heir: How so?

Artist: Look at the followers of great artists or philosophers. They're almost never as great as those they follow.

Sage: We're talking about epigones? The imitators?

Artist: Yes, of course.

Sage: The great one clears a path, but the others merely follow in the opened way?

Artist: That's the way of it.

Heir: Do the epigones think they're great?

Artist: I think most of them know they're not as great as the one they follow. But do they think they know more than most? Of course.

Director: Do they know more than most?

Artist: About some things? They might. But that's not the point.

Heir: What is the point?

Artist: The point becomes clear when they try to teach.

Heir: Teach? Why when they teach?

Artist: Because they have nothing to teach but what they've learned from the master.

Sage: But is that really so bad?

Artist: If you're not teaching from what you've learned on your own, you really have nothing worthwhile to say.

Heir: So what are you saying? No one can learn from anyone else and have something worthwhile to say?

Artist: No, no — of course not. But when you learn from another, you must make what you learn your own. Epigones don't do that, not in any meaningful sense. They simply parrot what the master said, with a few not-so-helpful embellishments of their own.

- Youth (Director, Heir)

Director: So what's the song I heard you talking about?

Heir: It's the one on now. It's called 'Young 'til I Die'.

Director: Is this is a sort of anthem to you?

Heir: Yes, and it always has been.

Director: And yet you're still young.

Heir: Of course. But what are you saying?

Director: How do you know you can stay young even when you're old?

Heir: I've seen others do it, Director. And you, if you'll pardon the personal reference, seem well on your way to being young until you die, too!

Director: Thank you, Heir. But are we young as a whole, or are we young in parts when we get old?

Heir: What do you mean?

Director: I mean, the body, it gets old. No?

Heir: Of course — parts of it, at least.

Director: So you're not saying your whole body will stay young?

Heir: No, of course not.

Director: Then here's the question that really interests me. What parts of the body stay young in those who stay young until they die?

Heir: The parts that make up the spirit.

Director: The fighting spirit or some other sort of spirit?

Heir: The fighting spirit.

Director: What tempers the fighting spirit? Or doesn't it need to be tempered?

Heir: No, it needs to be tempered. And it's the intellect that does it.

Director: Then let's hope our intellects don't age beyond the fight.

- Shame (Artist, Director, Heir)

Director: Heir, you've got quite a playlist of music here. What's this song now?

Heir: It's called 'Wiser Time'.

Directory: My, what an appropriate name. What's that first lyric? Something about no time for shame? But what does that mean?

Heir: When you've matured, Director, you realize that shame can debilitate you. So you move on.

Director: Do you forget the shame?

Heir: I don't know. I've never had any. Ha, ha. But seriously, I suppose it would be hard to forget.

Director: So you remember and yet move on?

Heir: That seems to be the way of it.

Director: But then we have shame in our baggage. Does that sound good?

Artist: Of course it doesn't sound good! You have to leave that baggage behind.

Heir: But how can you forget your shame?

Artist: As the song says — you have to learn there's simply no time.

Heir: But doesn't that seem somehow wrong?

Artist: Ha! Is it right to allow pointless old shame to smother the spirit?

Heir: Well, smothering doesn't sound so good.

Artist: Yes. But don't worry. You can make yourself feel better about the absence of this shame by forgiving others a similar shame of their own.

Heir: And will they in turn forgive the absence in you?

Artist: Of course not.

Heir: Why?

Artist: Because in that — there's nothing to forgive.

- Timelessness (Artist, Heir)

Heir: Do you think wisdom can be timeless?

Artist: No.

Heir: Why not?

Artist: Because all wisdom is of the here and now, and the here and now is of this thing and that.

Heir: And 'this thing and that' can never partake in timelessness?

Artist: Never. Oh, but don't look so concerned. You can get some of your 'timelessness' by looking back into the past and finding support for the wisdom you believe in now.

Heir: So we just use the past like that?

Artist: Yes, we do. Did you have any doubt?

Heir: Of course I had doubt! Don't we search the past to find the truth?

Artist: Whose truth do you think we're looking for when we do?

Heir: Be honest. You really don't think we can find timeless truth?

Artist: I really don't. Nor timeless wisdom, either.

Heir: But surely there's some sort of wisdom that's wise no matter the times.

Artist: I've never found it.

Heir: But you haven't looked. You're too busy with your art!

Artist: Oh, Heir. You didn't know me before I became an artist. I sought this wisdom you now seek, for years and years. I tortured myself looking for even a crumb that could lead me on.

Heir: And what did you find?

Artist: I found I was better served by art. As you'll be better served by politics.

Heir: A politics absent timeless wisdom? Well, we'll just have to wait and see what that brings.

~ Relativity (Artist, Director, Heir, Sage)

Artist: Is all wisdom relative to the person you're dealing with?

Heir: In other words, should we say different things to different people?

Artist: Yes. Sage, what do you think?

Sage: I think we share more with certain people and less with others.

Artist: And, Director, you agree?

Director: Actually, I'm inclined to think we should say the same things to everyone.

Sage: Always?

Director: Yes, always.

Artist: But that's what Director says. What do you think he does?

Sage: I think if he says it, he does it.

Director: Thank you for your confidence, Sage.

Sage: Besides, how would we know if it's otherwise?

Heir: Well, I suppose the one to whom he said something different could tell us all what he said.

Sage: Yes, but then it's Director's word against theirs. And whose word would you take?

Heir: Director's, of course.

Artist: Even if he might be lying to you?

Heir: I would trust that, even so, he had good reason to lie.

Artist: But wouldn't you want to know that good reason?

Heir: Of course I would, Artist. But how would I know I'd want to know? I'd believe the lie!

Director: But if you didn't?

Heir: I'd hound you — until I had the truth.

~ Love (Artist, Heir)

Artist: Love? Ha! I can tell you all about love.

Heir: Then tell me about this. Is there any such thing as wisdom when in love?

Artist: Absolutely not.

Heir: I always hear that. And yet I'm not so sure it's true.

Artist: How wouldn't it be true?

Heir: You could love someone but not give yourself over completely.

Artist: Why would you want to do that?

Heir: Because you want to keep a little reserve.

Artist: What, a reserve of wisdom? And what will you do? Sneak out in the dead of night and exercise this wisdom of yours all on your own? What good will that do you with your love?

Heir: Do you think you should share the wisdom?

Artist: Yes.

Heir: But you said there's no such thing as wisdom when in love!

Artist: Who says I think there is? When lovers 'share', they storm each other's citadel of wisdom, wisdom and its reserve.

Heir: And do what?

Artist: Raze it to the ground.

Heir: But why?

Artist: Because it stands in the way of their furious love!

Heir: So you just hand your reserve of wisdom over to be destroyed?

Artist: If the love is truly unbridled? Yes. Oh, but don't worry.

Heir: Why not?

Artist: You can always find more wisdom in the ashes — when the passion cools.

~ Friendship (Director, Heir)

Heir: Artist tells me I should give up on any hope of wisdom if I want to have all consuming love.

Director: Well, all consuming is all consuming. Or do you think wisdom is the exception, Heir?

Heir: I don't know. I suppose it's not.

Director: Then if wisdom doesn't go with that kind of love, what does it go with?

Heir: Sometimes I think it goes with nothing.

Director: And why would that be? Are you forgetting you can share your wisdom with good friends?

Heir: Do you really think I can? I mean, truly share?

Director: Wisdom? Absolutely. That's, in essence, what friends are for.

Heir: That's not how most people look at friends.

Director: You're not most people. So what do you think? If you had wisdom, would you share it with me?

Heir: Of course I would. Would you?

Director: Beyond a doubt.

Heir: Would you say wisdom can cement a friendship?

Director: I'd say it certainly can.

Heir: What would stop it from doing so?

Director: Too many imperfections in the glue, as it were.

Heir: Like what?

Director: Vanity, lack of confidence, half-truths — things like that.

Heir: You and I don't have those things.

Director: True. Now all we need is wisdom, and we're all set.

~ Awakening (Director, Sage)

Sage: We awaken when we come to wisdom.

Director: What does it feel like?

Sage: Oh, but you know, Director.

Director: You think I'm wise?

Sage: You have all the makings of someone who's wise.

Director: I don't know, Sage. What makes you say that?

Sage: Well, for one, you don't force yourself into the conversation. You always let others speak their minds.

Director: Okay. What else?

Sage: When you do speak, you often ask people to expand on what they've said or to clarify.

Director: And this is wise?

Sage: Yes, of course.

Director: So I must be awake? Or can you awaken and then go back to sleep?

Sage: Once awake, you stay awake.

Director: Even if you start to do unwise things? Or do the awakened never do such things?

Sage: Well, the wise certainly can make mistakes. So, yes, I suppose they can fall asleep at times.

Director: But then do they always wake back up? Or do some slumber on?

Sage: Once wise, you always wake back up.

Director: But what is it that wakes you up? A loud noise? Someone shaking you? What?

Sage: The best and most gentle is the rising sun on your face. Or else your beloved whispering softly in your ear. And I'm sure you can imagine other things like this.

~ Irony (Director, Sage)

Sage: Everyone talks about irony, but who really knows what it is?

Director: Are you talking about irony in the original, classical sense?

Sage: Yes. But what do you think classical irony is?

Director: It's simulated ignorance.

Sage: Right. The ironic used to dissemble.

Director: True, if we think of 'dissemble' in a very broad sense.

Sage: Why do you think they did this, dissemble, that is?

Director: I don't know, Sage. I've often wondered that myself. I mean, can dissembling ever be good?

Sage: No, I don't think it can.

Director: Then let me ask you this. Can dissembling ever be wise?

Sage: You draw a distinction between 'good' and 'wise'?

Director: Don't you think that distinction exists in fact? Can't you be good but not wise?

Sage: Yes, but I have trouble with being wise but not good.

Director: Well, why not say the wise dissemble and dissembling can be good?

Sage: You're going to have to give me an example.

Director: Okay. Suppose someone breaks into your home and demands the combination to your safe. You tell them you can't remember though you can.,

Sage: But that's not being ironic. That's just lying. Can you think of another?

Director: What about this? A child shows you a piece of artwork from school. It's awful, but you smile and say it's wonderful. You dissemble. No?

Sage: That's not dissembling. The artwork is in fact wonderful.

Director: Well, you have a point. So it seems I'm at a loss.

Sage: Yes, so it seems.

~ Tolerance (Director, Sage)

Director: Tell me, Sage. Is tolerance part of wisdom?

Sage: Oh yes, very much so.

Director: What should we tolerate?

Sage: New ideas, different opinions, strange customs — things like that.

Director: And what shouldn't we tolerate?

Sage: Poor behavior.

Director: Can you give me an example?

Sage: Of course. Being rude.

Director: What does it mean to be rude?

Sage: To be ill-mannered.

Director: But aren't manners, essentially, customs?

Sage: Well, yes.

Director: And didn't we say we should tolerate strange customs?

Sage: Yes, but certain manners are universal.

Director: In all times and places? Really?

Sage: Then you tell me, Director. What do you think we shouldn't tolerate?

Director: Harm done to us or our friends.

Sage: Oh, but what is harm?

Director: Anything that detracts from our well-being.

Sage: But how do you know what well-being is?

Director: And you have a reputation for wisdom, even though you don't know what well-being is? Or are you just playing with me?

Sage: As you were playing with me.

- Restraint (Artist, Director)

Artist: He thought you were playing with him? Were you?

Director: No. I honestly wanted the answers to my questions.

Artist: Some people don't understand that.

Director: Why not?

Artist: Because they expect people to be more restrained in their questioning.

Director: Why?

Artist: Because people feel like questions are an attack.

Director: An attack on what?

Artist: On them!

Director: But what is 'them'?

Artist: If I didn't know you better, I'd say you were playing with me!

Director: I'm not, Artist. What is it that I'm attacking with my questions?

Artist: Their opinions.

Director: But what if we can replace opinion with knowledge through our discussion?

Artist: Maybe people don't want knowledge.

Director: But do you really believe that? Doesn't everyone want knowledge?

Artist: If they do, Director, then why don't they feel good about going along with your questions?

Director: Maybe it's a painful process?

Artist: Ha! Then that's all the more reason for you to show restraint!

Director: But why don't my questions bother you?

Artist: Because I don't take you too seriously. And yet despite, or because of, my stance — I'm one of your better friends.

~ Harmony (Artist, Director, Heir)

Heir: I think the problem is not so much the pain of replacing opinion with knowledge. It's more a problem of a lack of harmony.

Director: I'm not very musical. In fact, some have called me amusical. So how can I expect to have harmonious conversations?

Heir: Don't you know when you agree and when you don't?

Director: Of course.

Heir: Well, then you know when you're being harmonious.

Director: But what if I don't disagree? What if I just question?

Heir: It depends how you question.

Director: Can you explain?

Heir: Yes, of course, Director. And what you just asked is a harmonious question, mostly.

Director: Why only mostly?

Heir: Because some people don't want to explain.

Director: So I have to know what they want before I ask?

Artist: Ha! Director has a point.

Heir: You don't think you can tell what they want?

Director: If I can, is it fair to them?

Heir: Why wouldn't it be?

Director: Because I'd be stereotyping them. I'd assume that certain types of people like certain types of questions, while other types loathe certain types of questions.

Heir: And you can't go beyond the stereotype toward knowledge without questioning them freely, questioning them however you will?

Director: Yes, and they should feel free to question me. And who knows? Our mutual questioning just might produce a sort of harmony of its own.

- Dissonance (Artist, Director)

Artist: The ignorant harmonize with each other.

Director: Oh, I don't know about that.

Artist: Why not?

Director: Because ignorance always sounds a dissonant note.

Artist: Even among its own?

Director: Yes, and even by itself.

Artist: You're saying we can't be in harmony with ourselves if we're ignorant?

Director: Yes. Ignorance ruins all private harmony.

Artist: But what about in public? I mean, if there are many others, others not ignorant, thriving in harmony — can one dissonant note ruin it all?

Director: The dissonant note will always stand out. So I think the answer is yes.

Artist: Then those in harmony will always have an interest in suppressing dissonance.

Director: Why, no. Their interest isn't to suppress. It's to teach.

Artist: Bah. It's easier to suppress than teach.

Director: But don't you think there will be a stronger harmony if they teach?

Artist: Yes, yes, Director. But if we're talking about teaching, why not look at it the other way round?

Director: The dissonant one teaches the others? How can ignorance teach?

Artist: But that's the thing. It might not be ignorance. The dissonant one might simply be playing in a different key.

Director: Ah, a different key. So it's not just ignorant noise?

Artist: Exactly.

Director: Then we who know the truth about this key will have to prove its worth to others. Which means we'll have to transpose, and bring it closer to home.

- Nature (Artist, Director, Heir, Sage)

Heir: Do you think people can be wise by nature?

Sage: No, we must all learn to be wise.

Artist: But aren't some natures better at learning than others?

Sage: How would we know?

Artist: How would we know? Ha! How wouldn't we know?

Sage: Well yes, we can tell someone has a better nature for learning something like math, for instance. But for learning to be wise?

Heir: Sage has a point. Math and wisdom are two very different things.

Director: But, Heir, are we good at learning math by nature, or do we have to learn how to learn it?

Artist: Yes, yes. But what are you saying? Some of us have natures that allow us to learn how to learn things more quickly. We can't get away from my point.

Sage: You might be right, Artist. But we haven't talked about the most important thing. Effort. That's what it takes to be wise.

Heir: And as far as effort is concerned, we're all made from the same clay?

Sage: Exactly. Effort is effort, no matter anything else.

Heir: And if effort is what makes us wise...

Sage: ...wisdom is open to all.

Director: But what effort does it take to be wise?

Sage: The effort to judge correctly.

Artist: Judge what correctly, Sage?

Sage: Other people and ourselves.

Artist: But what's to judge about us and them?

Sage: The effort we and they make.

~ Animals (Heir, Sage)

Heir: Do you think animals can be wise?

Sage: No.

Heir: Why not?

Sage: Only humans can be wise.

Heir: What does it mean for a human to be wise?

Sage: It means to know we're all made from the same clay. And to fully understand what that means and implies.

Heir: Aren't animals all made from the same clay?

Sage: I suppose.

Heir: But it's not the human clay?

Sage: That's right.

Heir: But what if clay is clay?

Sage: We're stretching the metaphor too far.

Heir: But if we look at the building blocks of life, humans and animals have the same stuff.

Sage: So that makes you think animals can be wise? Then no doubt there are degrees of wisdom.

Heir: I like that, yes. And that means some humans are wiser than others. But can't that also mean some animals are wiser than certain humans?

Sage: We can say that. But don't you think humans at their wisest are wiser than any animal can be?

Heir: I don't know. But do you know what I recommend?

Sage: No, what?

Heir: That we spend some time with animals and see.

~ Elders (Director, Heir)

Heir: I was taught to respect my elders.

Director: You were brought up well.

Heir: But not all elders deserve my respect.

Director: Why not?

Heir: Well, what are we supposed to respect in elders?

Director: Their wisdom.

Heir: And what makes an elder wise?

Director: Experience.

Heir: But you can have lots of experience and never grow wise.

Director: Why do you think that is? In other words, how do you transform experience into wisdom?

Heir: You have to digest it.

Director: But what does it mean to digest?

Heir: To make it a part of you.

Director: But surely all experience is part of us. Or isn't it?

Heir: No, you have a point. So how do we learn from experience?

Director: We let experience challenge our assumptions.

Heir: That doesn't sound very difficult.

Director: Oh, but Heir — few things are more difficult in life.

Heir: Why?

Director: Because we often don't know we have assumptions to be challenged. And when we find out we do, and that some of them are wrong...

Heir: ...we realize we're unwise. But, Director — that's just what I'd respect!

~ Needs (Artist, Director, Sage)

Sage: Different people have different needs.

Director: And you try to meet them in their own way?

Sage: Precisely.

Artist: So you say more to one, and less to another.

Sage: As I've said. But, as I recall, Director wants to say the same things to all.

Director: That's because I'm not speaking to people's needs. I speak to my own.

Sage: Then it's a good thing you're not an adviser!

Artist: Yes, yes. But here's something I wonder, Sage. Do you say one thing to an advisee, and another about that advisee to others?

Sage: I don't discuss advisees with anyone else.

Director: Not even if you find it to be a very hard case?

Sage: Well, yes. Sometimes I seek advice from those I respect.

Artist: So you're not fully wise. You need help.

Sage: Of course I'm not fully wise. And yes, at times I need help.

Artist: But what if you and these people you respect, your help, conclude your advisee has such and such a problem — and you don't tell this person you think it's such and such a problem? Do you see what I'm getting at?

Sage: I do. But sometimes hearing what I think the problem is, in so many words, at the wrong time, might be overwhelming.

Artist: So you deceive your advisee into thinking it's something else?

Sage: No! We make stages along the way and then we rest. That's hardly deceit.

Artist: But what else is it when you don't disclose what something truly is?

Director: I think they sometimes call that prudence.

Sage: Yes, Director. And that's exactly what it is.

~ Honesty (Artist, Director, Heir, Sage)

Heir: Of course honesty isn't the best policy.

Director: Why not?

Heir: Because honesty shouldn't be a policy.

Director: What should it be?

Artist: I'll tell you what it often is — a mistake!

Sage: When is it a mistake?

Artist: When it gets thrown back in your face.

Heir: So how do you know when to be honest?

Artist: You test your interlocutor with little truths, ones that don't hurt so much if thrown back at you.

Heir: And eventually you open up?

Artist: Yes — if you're brave.

Director: Okay. But let's get back to the question. If honesty isn't a policy, what is it?

Heir: A relief.

Director: It's a burden to carry truth unshared?

Heir: Don't you think it is?

Sage: I know it is.

Heir: But I would have thought you of all people would share.

Sage: I try to share. Oh, how I try! But not everyone is ready for truth.

Director: So you give them less than truth?

Sage: I give them truth enough. And then I hope for opportunity to give them more.

Artist: Well, you have plenty of opportunity here with us.

Sage: You're right — I do. And I'm starting to feel relief.

~ Memory (Artist, Director, Heir, Sage)

Director: Sage, how important is memory? Can we be wise without it?

Sage: Without memory? What are you talking about? Of course we need memory — even if only in order to live.

Director: Yes, but that's basic memory. I'm wondering about something more.

Sage: Well, it's true. You do need something more in order to be wise.

Director: And do you need something more again, or is memory enough?

Sage: What do you mean?

Director: Do you need to know how to analyze your memories?

Heir: How so, Director?

Artist: Oh, I know what he means. He's talking about remembering, for instance, if someone says one thing one time and another thing another.

Heir: But what analysis does that take?

Artist: You have to consider and then conclude whether that person is forgetful, deceitful, or trying to make a point.

Sage: A point? What point?

Artist: That different contexts warrant different speech.

Heir: But who needs to make that point? It's obvious to all!

Director: Is it?

Heir: Who wouldn't it be obvious to?

Director: To me. Tell me. How many contexts do you think there are in the world?

Heir: As many as there are people — and more.

Director: Then isn't it no small feat to remember what you've said in different contexts, assuming you say different things? But if you say the same things to all, there's little to remember. And so, everything equal — isn't that best?

~ Forgetting (Heir, Sage)

Heir: What's worth forgetting? The bad things?

Sage: No, I think we should remember them, if only to support what we've learned from them.

Heir: What do you mean?

Sage: Do you agree we can learn from the bad?

Heir: Yes, of course.

Sage: How can we be sure of what we learn?

Heir: I'm not sure I follow.

Sage: If we experience bad things X, Y, and Z, and from them we conclude that A, B, and C are truths — what happens if we forget X, Y, and Z?

Heir: I don't know. What happens?

Sage: We no longer know why we think A, B, and C are truths. We just believe in them blindly. Do you see what I mean?

Heir: Yes, and I think that makes some sense. But then we should never forget anything that lends support to a truth, bad or good? How can we possibly do that?

Sage: We have two types of memory. Active and passive. We can store much more in passive memory than active, and that's where we keep many of our supporting memories.

Heir: How do we bring passive memories back?

Sage: Something triggers them.

Heir: But, Sage, shouldn't we be able to remember when we want, not just when we're triggered?

Sage: Well, tell me. Can we know what our triggers are?

Heir: Sometimes, yes. But often we're surprised.

Sage: Then sometimes we can seek our triggers and remember when we will. But other times support for truth — takes a little luck.

~ Suffering (Director, Heir)

Director: But, Heir, is this a topic of conversation for a party? And look what a party it's shaping up to be! Do you really think most of these people will stay through to breakfast tomorrow morning?

Heir: Many if not most. Though I wouldn't be surprised if it's most. After all, people need time to get know each other. And I'm giving them that time. But back to our topic — suffering. Do you think it makes you wise?

Director: Well, I think it's like any type of experience. You can learn from it.

Heir: Yes, but can you learn more from suffering than from other types of experience?

Director: More? I think it depends. But let me tell you why suffering seems different. It's because it insists.

Heir: Insists?

Director: Yes, it insists it get a place in the forefront of our thoughts. Other types of experience aren't as demanding. At least most of them aren't.

Heir: What lays equal or greater claim to the forefront of our thoughts?

Director: Love.

Heir: Ha, ha! It's true! But you know, Director, some people would say love is a sort of suffering.

Director: Shh! Don't let that be heard. Love certainly can involve suffering, especially if it's unrequited. But don't you think love is greater than suffering? Isn't love more?

Heir: It is, Director. It is. But are we saying we can learn more from love than from suffering?

Director: Don't you think that's what we should say?

Heir: I do. And that means love is the thing most likely to make us wise.

Director: If love is properly approached.

Heir: And what's the proper way?

Director: Whatever way it takes — so as not to lose your head.

~ Selfishness (Artist, Heir)

Artist: Love is the most selfish passion you can feel.

Heir: How so?

Artist: You want the other to care for you, to love you, and only you.

Heir: Exclusivity is selfish?

Artist: No doubt.

Heir: But it's a good kind of selfishness.

Artist: Do you think I don't know that? Ha! But you tell me, Heir. Good exactly in what sense?

Heir: In the sense of being wise.

Artist: Wise? How do you mean?

Heir: Well, what is wisdom?

Artist: Don't try and escape into some general question when I want to know why you think the selfishness of love is wise!

Heir: Can we agree wisdom is getting what you want?

Artist: Why not?

Heir: And with love you want the other?

Artist: Yes.

Heir: Well, if selfishness drives you on to win the one you love, can't we say it's wise?

Artist: You're quite the sophist. But what does it mean to 'win' the one you love?

Heir: To have your love returned exclusively.

Artist: But what if your love is returned, but not exclusively?

Heir: And we're talking about romantic love? Your selfishness will drive you mad.

Artist: Then in that case, isn't it better not to be selfish — or not to love at all?

- Contemplation (Director, Sage)

Director: Do you think the wise lead a contemplative life?

Sage: There's no simple answer to that question.

Director: Why not?

Sage: Because the wise certainly do contemplate. You can't arrive at wisdom without contemplation. But are their lives more contemplative than active? It all depends.

Director: On what?

Sage: Their circumstances.

Director: Really? What kind of circumstances lead to a contemplative life?

Sage: Complex circumstances.

Director: And simple circumstances lead to an active life?

Sage: Yes.

Director: But can't you cut through complex circumstances in order to live an active life?

Sage: Well, yes, I suppose. If you want to badly enough. But you'll be inclined toward contemplation.

Director: Hmm. And what about those inclined toward an active life? If they want a contemplative life badly enough, can they have it?

Sage: But why would they want it?

Director: Why, Sage, because they love to think!

Sage: Yes, Director, but you know you can have an active life and think.

Director: True. But isn't it a question of degree? Isn't there more thinking in a contemplative life, by definition?

Sage: If contemplation were simply thinking, yes. But it's not always so. Sometimes it's being lost in reverie. And sometimes it's having your head in the clouds.

Director: Then here's what I say. The wise think. And whether they think in the course of an active life or one of contemplation — doesn't matter at all.

~ Solitude (Artist, Heir)

Heir: I love solitude.

Artist: Ha! Says the man who throws the biggest party I've ever seen.

Heir: No, but really, Artist. I do.

Artist: What do you do in your solitude?

Heir: What do you do in yours?

Artist: I work.

Heir: Well, I can't claim that I work.

Artist: So what do you do?

Heir: I enjoy myself.

Artist: How?

Heir: I enjoy my own company.

Artist: So you talk to yourself?

Heir: Haven't you ever heard of internal dialogue?

Artist: I certainly have. Are your conversations long or short?

Heir: It depends. Sometimes I go on and on for hours. But sometimes I get stuck.

Artist: You just keep on repeating the same things over and over again?

Heir: Yes, but then I often have a breakthrough.

Artist: And then you're free to talk on and on for hours once more?

Heir: I am. Don't you do this sort of thing?

Artist: I do. But I involve more characters than myself. And I write it all down.

Heir: But then your conversations aren't free.

Artist: That may be true to some extent. But I make up for it. I populate my solitude with friends.

~ Wholeness (Artist, Director, Heir, Sage)

Sage: It takes community to make us whole.

Director: What sort of community?

Sage: Good community.

Artist: And what is good community?

Sage: Any community that makes us whole.

Director: How do we know we're whole, Sage?

Sage: We can feel it. And there's no mistaking the feeling.

Director: So if we feel we're whole, that's it? We're whole?

Sage: Of course.

Director: But what if someone who says they feel whole doesn't seem whole to us?

Sage: How do you mean?

Director: I mean, we can just tell they're not whole.

Heir: Can you say more? How can we tell they're not whole?

Director: Through what they say.

Artist: Ha! And let me guess. They contradict themselves.

Director: Yes.

Heir: So you're saying we're not whole unless our community enables us to speak without contradiction?

Director: I am.

Heir: But, Director, that's an awfully high standard to set.

Director: It is, Heir. But wholeness is hard to achieve.

Sage: But why is contradiction the thing that matters?

Director: Because when we're whole, everything is of a piece.

~ Nations (Artist, Director)

Artist: Tell me, Director. What's the difference between political wisdom and the rest of wisdom?

Director: There is no difference.

Artist: But how can that be true?

Director: Why wouldn't it be true?

Artist: Because public life requires political wisdom while private life requires apolitical wisdom.

Director: Apolitical wisdom? You mean private life is somehow radically separated from public life?

Artist: Yes, of course.

Director: But I'm not sure that's so.

Artist: Why not?

Director: Well, what do you think political life is?

Artist: Life as shaped by the state.

Director: Shaped by the state, or shaped by the nation?

Artist: What difference does it make?

Director: The nation is more comprehensive than the state. It's the sum of both the public and private. Or isn't that so?

Artist: No, that's so.

Director: So tell me. If you wish to maintain the sum, can you separate the parts?

Artist: Of course not.

Director: Then, in a nation, there's no radical separation of public and private?

Artist: I suppose there isn't, if the nation really is the sum.

Director: If it is, then I think you see why I'm inclined to say — all wisdom is the same.

- Inheritance (Artist, Director, Heir, Sage)

Artist: Wisdom can't be inherited.

Heir: What can be inherited?

Artist: Besides physical traits? Money, and things, and certain opinions.

Heir: But what if those opinions are wise?

Artist: They may have been wise for the one who held them. But to pass them on? There's no wisdom in that.

Sage: Why not?

Artist: Because, Sage, circumstances change.

Sage: And opinions have to do with circumstances, essentially?

Artist: Yes, of course.

Sage: But what if the circumstances haven't changed?

Artist: Circumstances always change. If only from one person to another.

Sage: Yes, but there are personal circumstances and then there are greater circumstances, circumstances that don't change as often as the personal.

Artist: Ha! So you're saying if you inherit opinions that deal well with the greater circumstances, you can be wise as far as that goes?

Sage: Yes.

Director: Tell me, Sage. Does it do any good to be wise concerning greater circumstances if you're not wise concerning personal things?

Sage: Sometimes great leaders are exactly that way.

Director: Are they happy?

Sage: Happy that they've got the greater things right? Yes.

Heir: No, but are they happy, truly happy?

Artist: I'll answer for Sage with a question: How could they be?

- Alike (Director, Heir, Sage)

Sage: Wisdom is proof against luck.

Director: Bad luck, you mean?

Sage: Yes, of course. When you're wise, you can anticipate things and ward them off.

Heir: But what if they're not what you thought they were?

Sage: Knowing what they are is part of being wise.

Heir: But how can you know, really know, if you don't experience them, if you ward them off?

Sage: You experience other things like them, and know.

Heir: But are any two things really alike?

Director: I think Heir has a point, Sage.

Sage: Yes, but it takes wisdom to know if things are like enough.

Heir: So how about an example? If a dog bites me, does wisdom say all dogs are like enough — all dogs are bad?

Sage: Wisdom says the ones like the one that bit you are bad.

Heir: But how will I know which ones are like the one that bit? Doesn't that take a bit of luck?

Sage: What do you mean?

Heir: I mean, can I really know a dog is a biting dog unless I have the luck to see it bite?

Sage: Yes, but there are signs preceding every dog's bite.

Heir: And if we see the signs, we know enough? Barking and snarling and so on?

Sage: Right. The signs are always the same. So once you've seen them, you know.

Director: But are they the same? What about the dog whose bark is worse than its bite?

Sage: Oh, Director, there are always exceptions. But why take a chance you're dealing with one?

~ Peace (Artist, Director, Heir, Sage)

Sage: The wise are always at peace.

Artist: Even in the midst of a tumult? Or will you tell us the wise know how to steer clear of trouble?

Heir: I think even the wise get caught up in events at times.

Sage: And when they do, they maintain their peace.

Artist: How? By not taking trouble seriously?

Sage: Of course they take trouble seriously — but not too seriously.

Director: What would it mean to take trouble too seriously?

Sage: To dwell on it to the point where it cripples. In fact, it's better not to dwell on it at all.

Director: It's best to think, act, and then move on?

Sage: Exactly so.

Artist: Yes, yes — but what if you can't move on? What if you're stuck?

Sage: If you have to be stuck, isn't it better to be at peace?

Heir: But who says you have to be stuck?

Director: What's the way not to be?

Heir: The way is to fight.

Artist: Even if that means losing your peace?

Heir: There's no reason we can't be at peace in our souls as we fight to be free.

Director: Sage, what do you think of that?

Sage: I think Heir is very young.

Artist: Ha! So you don't accept his paradox of fighting in peace?

Sage: Oh, I do. But I'm not always so sanguine we'll win.

- War (Artist, Director, Heir, Sage)

Artist: When the wise wage war, do they do so with words?

Sage: Mostly they do so through silence.

Artist: What kind of war is that?

Sage: One that's often deadly.

Director: Deadly in what sense?

Sage: In the sense that it makes the other feel like he or she has ceased to exist.

Heir: I think Sage is making an excellent point. If someone wise ignored me, I'd feel awful.

Artist: But if you were at war with this person, would you really think they're wise?

Director: Yes, Artist, that's a good point. But what if your enemy is generally reputed to be wise?

Artist: I'd fight the reputation. And if I had success with that, I think our wise one would have something to say.

Sage: You think the wise care that much about their reputations?

Director: What do they care about, Sage?

Sage: Wisdom itself.

Artist: Tell us how you can be wise if you're thought to be unwise.

Director: Artist, are you forgetting? Surely you know of times when it's best to play dumb.

Artist: Well, yes, that's true.

Director: So it's fine for Sage to say he cares about wisdom itself.

Heir: But then won't he lose his major weapon in the fight? I mean, why should I care if I'm ignored by what to all appearances is a fool?

Sage: Ah, but now you're forgetting something, Heir. Don't you think you'd be wise enough to know I'm no fool? And wouldn't you be honest enough to care?

~ Pleasure (Director, Sage)

Director: Sage, have you ever heard that the purpose of wisdom is to obtain pleasure?

Sage: I have. But I don't agree.

Director: What is the purpose of wisdom?

Sage: To help you live a good life.

Director: What's a good life?

Sage: Oh, you know. One filled with friends and successes and so on.

Director: But not pleasures?

Sage: Well, yes, of course — pleasures, too. But why are you insisting on pleasure?

Director: Because I find it hard to get away from.

Sage: What do you mean?

Director: Look at your answer to my question about the good life. You mentioned friends and successes. Don't both friends and successes bring us pleasure?

Sage: True.

Director: So my question is: Are there any things pertaining to a good life that don't bring us pleasure?

Sage: Here's where you're going wrong, Director. You fail to distinguish between pleasure and joy.

Director: Ah, I knew I was going wrong somewhere. What's the difference between the two?

Sage: Pleasure is superficial while joy is profound.

Director: And there are joys with friends? And success brings us joy?

Sage: Yes, now you understand.

Director: Then we can say with confidence that the purpose of wisdom is joy?

Sage: We can. And we're right.

~ Purpose (Artist, Heir)

Artist: Just listen to those two. Wisdom and joy. Ha!

Heir: What's wrong with wisdom and joy?

Artist: If joy is the only aim of your wisdom, you're helpless.

Heir: Helpless? What are you talking about?

Artist: You just hope to float from joy to joy, not taking into account something much more serious. Or do you think joy is the serious business of life?

Heir: I guess I've never thought about it before. But what's this more serious thing you're talking about?

Artist: Power.

Heir: Ah, I see. And that should be your aim in life?

Artist: No, of course not. But if you want to win your joy, you need power. Do you need a remedial lesson from me on why this is so?

Heir: No, I think I understand why. But we're talking about power in a very broad sense.

Artist: We're talking about power in the broadest possible sense.

Heir: Okay. But then what are we saying? That the purpose of wisdom is to obtain power for the sake of joy?

Artist: Almost. We can't forget about the thing our friends dismissed. Pleasure.

Heir: So it's wisdom for power for pleasure and joy?

Artist: Can it be anything else?

Heir: That sounds about right to me.

Artist: Yes. But there's one thing I should mention, something about joy.

Heir: What?

Artist: It takes a twofold wisdom. Wisdom to win it, as we've said. But when you have it, you need wisdom not to let it — go to your head.

~ Compromise (Artist, Director, Heir, Sage)

Director: When do the wise compromise and when do they not?

Sage: Oh, Director, there's no simple answer to that question.

Heir: But can't we say they never compromise in matters of principle?

Sage: Yes, people often say that. But what does it mean?

Heir: It means you always live up to your beliefs.

Sage: Then you'd better be very sure about those beliefs.

Director: How do we become sure? By believing in something for a long time?

Heir: We become sure by thinking things through.

Director: And when we think things through, do we always think them through well?

Heir: Always? Of course not.

Director: But, still, we should live up to what we think?

Heir: We need to think well before we do that.

Sage: And where are we if we don't think well? Without principles?

Heir: Well, it's a problem.

Artist: Ha! It certainly is. So which is better? To live according to principles that aren't true, or to live without principles?

Heir: Oh, Artist, I don't know. Don't we all need principles?

Director: If that's true, and the principles aren't, isn't that a sort of compromise?

Heir: But how is it a compromise if you don't know your principles are false?

Sage: You compromise unconsciously.

Artist: I'd prefer to compromise consciously.

Heir: Who wouldn't?

Artist: Those who don't like to think.

~ Ideas (Director, Heir, Sage)

Director: What's an idea?

Heir: Do you mean in a philosophical sense?

Director: No, just in a general sense.

Heir: I suppose it's a notion.

Director: And what's a notion?

Heir: A conception, or a belief.

Director: Sage, do you agree?

Sage: I think an idea is more complex a thing. But I'm fine with what we're saying.

Director: Okay. So here's what I want to know. Do the wise have many ideas or few?

Heir: I think the wise have many ideas.

Director: Would you say you can't be wise without many ideas?

Heir: Yes.

Sage: Oh but, Heir! Of course you can be wise with few ideas. You could have a great many ideas and they could all be bad. But if you have a few good ones, and you stick to them, you can certainly be wise.

Director: How do we know if our ideas are good?

Sage: It's easier to know if our ideas are bad. Bad ideas bring bad results.

Director: Results?

Sage: Yes, in life.

Heir: But why is it easier to know ideas are bad? Don't good ideas bring good results? And then can't we know them for what they are?

Sage: Yes, Heir, but there's a problem here. People want us to share our good ideas. But what's good for us might not be good for them. And if our ideas bring bad results for others, won't it be harder for us to see these ideas as good?

~ Convictions (Artist, Director, Heir, Sage)

Artist: Convictions? Ha! Of course I know what convictions are. What makes you ask, Sage?

Sage: Sometimes you act as if you don't have any.

Artist: And if I don't have any then that means I also never have the courage of my convictions?

Sage: It would seem to follow.

Director: Why don't you tell us what a conviction is, Artist?

Artist: It's a firmly held opinion or belief.

Director: So it doesn't have to do with knowledge?

Artist: Of course it doesn't. Opinions and beliefs are the two things you have precisely when you don't know.

Director: Hmm. Is there such a thing as the courage of your knowledge?

Artist: Absolutely! And I'm glad you brought this up. People who know are often afraid to speak up, to share their knowledge.

Director: Why do you think that is?

Artist: Because they don't want to ruffle people's convictions.

Heir: What happens when you ruffle people's convictions?

Artist: They want to ruffle something in turn. And since knowledge doesn't ruffle — they want to ruffle you!

Heir: But what if people's convictions square nicely with your knowledge?

Artist: Ah, then something wonderful might happen. You might witness a transformation of conviction into knowledge — assuming you speak up.

Heir: So those transformed go from saying 'I believe' to 'I know'?

Artist: Yes, but it's much more than a change in what they say. It's a change in who they are.

~ Unrequited (Director, Sage)

Sage: I think wisdom and philosophy can support one another nicely.

Director: Because philosophy loves wisdom?

Sage: Yes.

Director: But, Sage, does it go the other way, too? Does wisdom love philosophy?

Sage: Who doesn't love to be loved?

Director: An interesting answer. One that means philosophy likely suffers unrequited love!

Sage: Oh, you can love to be loved and still love. But why are you worried about this?

Director: Don't you know lovers always worry about things like this? They hang on every word their beloved speaks.

Sage: But why?

Director: Ah, you're teasing. But I'll answer. Lovers want to see if their love is returned.

Sage: What happens if wisdom returns philosophy's love?

Director: I'm not sure. I don't think it's ever happened before.

Sage: Oh, come on! It must have happened. And I think it would make philosophy's love grow stronger.

Director: And would that make wisdom's love grow stronger?

Sage: Yes.

Director: So we're talking about reciprocal, mutually supportive love?

Sage: We are.

Director: I don't believe it. Philosophy has been spurned too often before.

Sage: And philosophy has never spurned wisdom?

Director: Never.

Sage: Well, that only makes loyal, steadfast philosophy — all the more worthy of love.

- Courage (Artist, Director, Heir)

Heir: I really like the idea of having the courage of your knowledge.

Artist: What do you like about it?

Heir: It think it reflects both a profound internal and a profound external truth.

Artist: What truths are these?

Heir: You can't have knowledge in the first place unless you have courage. That's the internal truth. And then you have to have courage to live up to what you know. That's the external truth.

Director: Tell us, Heir. Why does it take courage to have knowledge?

Heir: Because you can't be afraid to think.

Director: What's frightening about thought?

Heir: You might have to change what you believe.

Director: And why is that change frightening?

Heir: Because often times we believe what's comforting rather than what's true.

Director: It takes courage to sacrifice comfort?

Heir: Of course it does. Don't you agree?

Director: Well, let me ask. Do comfort and courage ever go together?

Heir: I don't know. That seems counterintuitive.

Director: Look at it this way. We form habits, yes?

Heir: Of course.

Director: And are we comfortable in our habits?

Heir: For the most part.

Director: What if we made a habit of courage? Could we find comfort in that?

Heir: Ah, Director — I like the way you think!

~ Cowardice (Artist, Heir)

Artist: I'll admit something to you, Heir. But I ask that you keep it in confidence. I'm a halfway coward. Can you guess in which way?

Heir: If I had to guess? I'd say you're courageous internally.

Artist: Yes. I'm not afraid to think and change my thoughts.

Heir: But why would you say you're a coward externally?

Artist: You know the answer. I don't live up to what I know.

Heir: But, Artist, what about your work? I would say what you create takes great courage!

Artist: You're young and in some ways naive.

Heir: But you put what you know into your work. Don't you?

Artist: Yes, of course.

Heir: So that must take courage. And I think it involves living up to what you know.

Artist: But what about me in person? That's where I lack courage. I'd rather make a smart quip than spell out in so many words just what I think.

Heir: Quips can reveal the truth.

Artist: Ah, you're a good friend to me.

Heir: Do you think I'm just saying that and don't really mean it?

Artist: No, I do think you mean it.

Heir: Then tell me why you're so intent on making yourself out to be a coward. Most people would do everything they can to make the opposite case.

Artist: I don't know. I guess I've never liked making my own case.

Heir: Yes, but I think it's something else. I think your standard is higher than most. So when you don't live up to it, you think you're a coward, even though you have courage enough.

Artist: Enough? Ha! Ha, ha! How happy I'd be if only I had — courage enough!

~ Alliances (Artist, Director, Heir, Sage)

Heir: I think the four of us make for a good alliance.

Director: One that allows you not to spend time with your other guests?

Heir: Ha, ha. Absence makes the heart grow fond.

Director: But too much absence makes the heart forget.

Heir: Then you know who I want to forget me not.

Sage: Why are we a good alliance, Heir?

Heir: Because we represent four important aspects of life. Artist, creativity. Director, philosophy. And you, Sage, wisdom.

Artist: And you?

Heir: Politics.

Artist: You have no doubt that's your way?

Heir: None.

Director: Well, that way involves money, my friend. So how much will you raise from this event?

Heir: Enough to get started.

Artist: We're at a fundraiser?

Heir: Ha, ha! I didn't want you to know! I couldn't possibly take any money from you, my starving artist friend.

Sage: And you let me off lightly, Heir.

Heir: I don't see why you insisted on making a contribution.

Sage: It's because I couldn't stand the thought of your taking money from strangers and not from me!

Heir: Oh, but they're not really strangers. They're my allies, of sorts. I say 'of sorts' because... well, you know why. There are allies and then there are allies! And my inner circle is here, my friends — with you.

~ Dirt (Artist, Director, Heir, Sage)

Artist: Your inner circle — yes, sure. But how am I in that circle if I don't know what's going on?

Heir: I wanted it to be a surprise! My very first fund raising event! And I'm honored you're here. So, Artist, don't be offended. Please?

Artist: Well, Heir, you must be glad you pulled off your first political coup. You kept me in the dark. I'm sure that skill will come in handy one of these days.

Director: Yes, I'm sure it will. But the first coup didn't have to do with you. The real first coup was Heir's deciding to run.

Heir: Yes, and the next will come through the money I raise here.

Artist: How will you use it?

Heir: We'll plot together, my friend, and figure that out.

Artist: If you ask me, you should use the money to strike at your enemies through all means both foul and fair.

Sage: Why foul?

Artist: Because that's what Heir's enemies are — and they should get what they deserve!

Sage: But won't he be foul if he uses foul means?

Artist: Ha! Not if he wears gloves.

Sage: But be serious. Should Heir really get dirty, gloves or not?

Artist: Yes. Dirt is very important in politics.

Heir: How so?

Artist: Dirt is earth, and earth is soil. And honest soil on the hands is just what voters like to see.

Sage: Well, there's nothing foul about soil.

Artist: Exactly. So do you see, Heir? You just have to put it a certain way — and you can come out clean.

~ Silence (Director, Sage)

Director: Well, Sage, you certainly know how to keep a secret. Artist had no idea.

Sage: Silence is one of the many skills of the wise.

Director: Aside from explicit promises to hold their tongue, when do the wise remain silent?

Sage: When silence is cutting, as we discussed.

Director: Yes, but are there other times?

Sage: Of course. One is when you're certain the other party won't understand.

Director: How can you be certain of that?

Sage: You lead your way up to the point in question, checking for comprehension along the way.

Director: And if there's comprehension, you just keep on going?

Sage: Yes.

Director: And this holds for everything? Even your innermost truth?

Sage: Well, I'm not sure about my innermost truths.

Director: You have more than one?

Sage: Don't we all?

Director: I must be missing out — because I only have one.

Sage: What is it?

Director: Oh, Sage! We're going to have to work our way toward it.

Sage: You'd check my comprehension each step along the way?

Director: Of course! I think you gave me excellent advice.

Sage: Then what's the first step?

Director: Ah, but when you're checking — that's exactly what you can't reveal.

~ Babble (Artist, Director, Heir)

Artist: You're going to have to learn how to babble, Heir.

Heir: And why do you say that?

Artist: Because people are going to expect you to fill the silences.

Director: Artist may have a point.

Heir: But why babble? Why not intelligent talk?

Artist: Ha! Do you think people are voting for intelligent talk?

Heir: Do you think they're voting for babble?

Director: What about these people here tonight? What do they want to hear you say?

Heir: That I'll give them what they want.

Director: And people will talk about what they want all through your campaign?

Heir: Mostly.

Director: So they don't want you to babble to them. They want you to make them promises.

Artist: Better the babble!

Heir: Ha, ha. But yes, Director, people will be trying to get me to make promises.

Director: Will you promise?

Heir: I'll have to.

Director: How will you decide what to promise?

Heir: I'll think it all out ahead.

Director: You mean you haven't done so already?

Heir: Well....

Director: And here you are in this lion's den of a party? Artist, what can we do to help?

Heir: Babble and babble and babble some more — until we force them all to go home!

~ Applause (Artist, Director, Heir, Sage)

Director: Heir, is there a way to check for comprehension when you speak to a crowd?

Heir: Comprehension? What's to comprehend? All that matters is their response.

Director: You mean their applause?

Heir: Of course!

Director: But why do they applaud?

Heir: They like what I have to say.

Director: And is what you have to say set to music?

Heir: Music? What do you mean?

Artist: Oh, I know what he means. He's talking about tone, emotional content, and so on.

Director: Yes. So what I'm wondering is this. Can you say the same things but get different responses depending on the quality of your tune?

Heir: No doubt. People don't like it when, for instance, you're flat.

Artist: Nor do they like it when you're sharp.

Director: So the crowd is expert in judging pitch?

Sage: I don't know that I'd call it expert, Director. It just knows what it likes.

Director: But then who's the expert? Who's to judge?

Heir: Why do we need someone to judge? All that matters is the tune's effect.

Director: The effect on the crowd?

Heir: What else?

Director: Well, doesn't the crowd sing back to you?

Heir: It does.

Director: Then your tune has an effect on their tune. And I, for one, intend to judge their tune's effect on you.

- Misunderstood (Artist, Heir)

Artist: I think you, as a politician, will have to get comfortable with being misunderstood. Did Sage ever tell you that?

Heir: No, he certainly never did. But why do you think I need to get comfortable with being misunderstood?

Artist: Because if certain people understood you, they wouldn't vote for you.

Heir: How do you know that?

Artist: Know? Ha! I know you and I know them.

Heir: But maybe you don't know what you think you know.

Artist: Well, tell me. Are you a simple soul, or are you more complex?

Heir: In many ways I'm simple. But I know what you mean. I'm more complex.

Artist: Are most people simple or are they complex?

Heir: I've often wondered that.

Artist: Then wonder some more, Heir — because the wrong answer here is a reef that can sink a political ship.

Heir: Do you think most people are simple?

Artist: I do.

Heir: And you're suggesting if I'm more complex, it would be hard for them to understand who I am? And we're not talking about my political message. We're talking about who I am as me?

Artist: The simple usually have a hard time understanding complexity. That's why you have to make it simple for them.

Heir: In my message, you mean?

Artist: Yes, that's how you can win. By keeping it very simple.

Heir: But even if I do that, I still want people to understand me for who I am.

Artist: Then let them understand you — as the one who'll win.

~ Worries (Director, Heir)

Heir: I'm not sure I can win.

Director: What's this? Why not?

Heir: Artist made it clear that I need to be prepared to be misunderstood throughout my campaign.

Director: Hmm. Are you always understood in your day-to-day life?

Heir: No.

Director: You mean every stranger you meet doesn't comprehend your essence, what you're all about?

Heir: Of course not.

Director: So why are you worried about the campaign? Won't it be similar? Some people will understand you. Many won't.

Heir: But do I want their vote if they don't understand me?

Director: Won't they understand what you stand for?

Heir: If I do a good job articulating that, yes.

Director: Then let them vote for what you stand for. Because, in the end, they're not voting for you — they're voting for themselves.

Heir: And what they see of them in me?

Director: Yes. But let me tell you. You've heard of trying to be all things to all people? Well, I don't recommend that. But you will be some things to some people, many people. And doesn't that mean they'll understand those things when they vote?

Heir: I suppose. But, psychologically, this is all a bit more complicated than it seems.

Director: That's because you're a thinker, Heir. Not all politicians are.

Heir: Do you think that's a disadvantage?

Director: No. But it means you have to learn how to use thought to your advantage.

Heir: There's nothing more I'd rather learn. So tell me what you know.

- Isolation (Director, Sage)

Director: Would the wise ever isolate themselves?

Sage: When in the process of growing wise, or once wise?

Director: Both.

Sage: Well, the wise sometimes isolate themselves when growing wise.

Director: Why do they do that?

Sage: They need time alone to build themselves up.

Director: And once built up?

Sage: They never isolate themselves again.

Director: Because they've learned all they can learn?

Sage: Of course not. But they have the foundation in place.

Director: And it's safe for them to build on that with others around?

Sage: Yes. In fact, I'd say it's when we're with others that we do most of the building.

Director: Through conversation?

Sage: Of course. And isn't that how it is with philosophers?

Director: Oh, but Sage. You know philosophers aren't wise.

Sage: You say that. But I don't believe it.

Director: How much building up have you seen me do? Do I have some theory or structure of ideas you can get a hold of to prove I'm wise?

Sage: I don't know you well enough to say. But I suspect you do.

Director: Why?

Sage: Because if you don't, then what's the point of your philosophy?

Director: But it's not 'my philosophy'. It's just... philosophy.

Sage: And that, my friend, only serves — to give the question force.

~ Moderation (Artist, Director, Heir, Sage)

Sage: And so, I agree with the ancient adage — nothing too much. Everything in moderation.

Artist: Including wisdom?

Heir: Ah, Artist! Count on you to ask that question.

Director: I was about to if he didn't.

Heir: Well, Sage, what do you say? Can you have too much wisdom?

Sage: Of course not. Wisdom is the one exception to the rule.

Artist: Is it? What about courage? Can you have too much of that?

Sage: Yes, if you're courageous to the point of being foolhardy.

Artist: But then you're foolhardy and not courageous. No?

Director: It seems we have two exceptions to the rule. Are there any others?

Artist: What about being strong? Can we ever be too strong?

Heir: Yes, and what about being just? Can we ever be too just?

Director: Maybe we need to take a step back and think about what moderation is intended to cover.

Sage: Yes, Director. Moderation covers temptations.

Director: Like too much food, too much wine? Things like that?

Sage: Those are exactly the sorts of things moderation covers.

Artist: What about lies? Aren't we often tempted to lie? Should we be moderate in that?

Sage: A moderate liar? Ha, ha. Sure, Artist. Why not?

Artist: But I'm serious. Does the concept of moderation apply to lies?

Heir: I think it does, in a way. If we lie for no good reason, it's always a lie too much. But if we lie for a good reason? Like to save our lives or the lives of friends? It's never too much. So we should lie in just the right amount, at just the right times. And be moderate.

~ Thinking (Director, Heir)

Director: Tell me, Heir. What do you hope to accomplish when you win?

Heir: When I win? Ha, ha! What makes you so confident?

Director: You make me so confident.

Heir: Well, I hope I make the voters confident, too!

Director: It's your race to lose. But you didn't answer my question.

Heir: What do I want to accomplish? I think you'll laugh.

Director: Try me.

Heir: I hope to make people think.

Director: Well, I'm not laughing. But I am puzzled. What do you want them to think about?

Heir: Everything! So long as they think.

Director: But what does thinking for the sake of thinking accomplish?

Heir: You of all people ask me that?

Director: Why do you say that?

Heir: Because you're the one who gave me the idea!

Director: How did I do that?

Heir: By making me think!

Director: And what was the end result of that?

Heir: I can't believe you're asking me this! I'd better tell you my full intent. You see, I hope, by making people think, to make a better world.

Director: Oh ho! I think that intent cloaks an unlimited ambition! A very dangerous thing.

Heir: Then why are you smirking?

Director: Because you're just the one to do it. To make a better world. That is, if it's possible to do it. And I have some serious doubts.

~ Opinions (Artist, Director, Heir)

Artist: But people don't think. They have opinions.

Heir: If that's true, then what's the best I can do?

Artist: Get them to change their opinions.

Heir: Oh, but Artist. Don't you know every time we change our opinions we have to think, if only a little?

Artist: Ha! If that's true then that 'if only a little' is very little indeed.

Heir: Director, what do you think about this?

Director: People's identity is often tied up with their opinions. So if you ask them to change an opinion you are, in a sense, asking them to change who they think they are.

Heir: So it's easier to get them to think without changing their opinions?

Director: Yes, I suppose. But then what's the point of thought?

Heir: So what are you saying I should do?

Artist: I'll tell you what you should do. Take people as they are and don't expect to change them.

Heir: And when I take them as they are, what do I do with them?

Artist: Lead them!

Heir: But lead them where?

Artist: Well, there are two basic options. One, you lead them where they want to go, according to their opinions. Or, two, you lead them where you want to go.

Heir: And I suppose you'll say it's impossible, or at least almost impossible, to lead them where I want to go, contrary to their opinions.

Artist: Of course.

Heir: So what if I compromise between the two?

Artist: Ah, but who's ever happy with that?

~ Validation (Artist, Director, Heir)

Artist: If you lead people to where you want to go, not where they want to go, you're going to get precious little validation.

Heir: They'll go kicking and screaming all the way?

Artist: Of course.

Heir: But what if you can put up with that? I mean, does a wise leader always need validation? And, for that matter, does a wise artist?

Artist: Well, you're asking a very good question. But let's forget about being wise. Do I need validation for my work? No.

Director: But then, Artist, how do you know what you're doing is worthwhile? Do you just have to believe?

Artist: No, I have proof.

Director: How?

Artist: I compare my work to that of others I admire.

Heir: But you have to be brutally honest, right?

Artist: That's the trick. If you are, and you still think your work isn't too bad, then by all means — carry on.

Heir: So I have to compare myself to leaders I admire? Leaders who went largely their own way despite pressure to go somewhere else?

Artist: Yes.

Director: But is it really the same in either case?

Artist: Why wouldn't it be?

Director: Artists with no validation can go on being artists. But leaders with no validation? Won't they of necessity cease to lead?

Artists: Oh, not necessarily. Think of tyrants.

Director: Yes, but when I do, I see how they need validation so badly they often force it from their subjects. So it seems all leaders need some. But freely given is best.

~ Trust (Artist, Director, Heir, Sage)

Artist: You don't think artists have to earn the trust of their audience?

Sage: Sure, Artist. But not as much as advisers have to earn the trust of those they advise.

Director: I don't know. Let's say we're talking about an author. What's more intimate, and therefore trusting, than the relationship between reader and book?

Heir: I think that's a great point. Sage, don't you agree?

Sage: I suppose. So we're saying books and advice require an equal amount of trust? But if that's true, it only holds for good books, very good books — excellent books.

Heir: Yes, of course. But, you know, it also holds for excellent leaders.

Director: What makes for the intimacy, the trust, between leader and led?

Heir: The thinking involved.

Director: You mean, if a leader causes you to think, that's as intimate as it gets?

Artist: Yes, yes — but you can think and still not trust.

Heir: Great leaders win your trust through how, how they make you think.

Artist: Okay, Heir. But how often are political thoughts as intimate as thoughts in a book?

Heir: Oh, I'd say they're often as intimate. They affect your life in every possible way.

Sage: So the three of us require trust for what we do. But what about philosophy?

Director: You doubt that it takes trust?

Sage: We're not sure what it takes. So tell us.

Director: Well, it certainly takes trust. But more than just trust in a philosopher.

Heir: Then trust in what?

Director: Trust in your own thoughts, Heir. The thoughts brought on in reaction to what you and a philosopher, together, say.

- Wariness (Director, Heir)

Heir: Director, tell me something. Do you think philosophers can lead?

Director: Yes and no.

Heir: I should have guessed that's what you'd say.

Director: Well, then you tell me. Do you think leaders can lead?

Heir: Ha, ha. Of course.

Director: What about artists?

Heir: To tell you the truth, I'd be wary of an artist that tried to lead.

Director: Even our Artist?

Heir: Yes.

Director: Why?

Heir: Because artists can get carried away by their own ideas.

Director: And leaders and philosophers can't?

Heir: What are you suggesting? We have to be wary of everyone?

Director: We must always be on guard.

Heir: I'm afraid that's true. But isn't that an awful way to live?

Director: Oh, I don't know. What does it mean to be wary?

Heir: To show caution.

Director: What's the opposite of caution?

Heir: Recklessness.

Director: When are you more successful? When you're cautious or reckless?

Heir: You're most successful when you're between the two. When you're bold.

Director: And is that what artists, and philosophers, and leaders should be?

Heir: Yes. And I always trust the bold — so long as they walk the line.

- Sorrow (Director, Heir, Sage)

Sage: Sorrow can lead to wisdom.

Heir: But you can be wise without sorrow, right?

Sage: Yes, but it's often harder.

Heir: Why?

Sage: Sorrow gives you insight.

Heir: And insight makes you wise?

Sage: Of course.

Director: But here's what I wonder, Sage. Can wisdom lead to sorrow?

Sage: It can.

Director: Then let me ask. Does wisdom always lead to sorrow?

Sage: Director, how could I possibly believe that?

Director: You could believe it if it's true. Is it?

Sage: No. Wisdom only sometimes leads to sorrow.

Director: Under what conditions?

Sage: Oh, who can say?

Director: Someone who's wise in the ways of wisdom.

Heir: Director, do you think wisdom must lead to sorrow?

Director: Necessarily? No.

Heir: Under what conditions would it?

Director: When you let your wisdom back you into a corner.

Heir: But it's not wise to do that.

Director: Meaning true wisdom would never corner you so?

Heir: Yes. And if you're cornered, you know you can't be wise.

- Rejoicing (Artist, Director, Heir)

Artist: The wise should rejoice.

Heir: For what?

Artist: For being wise!

Heir: But what if they're all alone in their wisdom?

Artist: We're always all alone in our wisdom.

Heir: You mean it's something we can't share?

Artist: Sharing wisdom presupposes that the other is already wise.

Heir: But people can learn.

Artist: Learn to be wise? Ha!

Heir: Why do you laugh?

Artist: Because we can learn this or that. But can we ever learn from others how to be wise?

Heir: Director?

Director: I think Artist has a point. In the end, learning to be wise is something we do on our own.

Heir: Even if we have a mentor?

Artist: Especially if we have a mentor!

Heir: Why especially?

Artist: Mentors can make you think you're wise when you're not.

Heir: Because you bask in their glow?

Artist: Yes.

Heir: But shouldn't we rejoice in any glow?

Artist: Sure, so long as we're aware it's no glow of our own.

~ Determination (Artist, Director, Heir)

Artist: It's not always wise to be determined.

Heir: Why not?

Artist: Circumstances change, and you need to adjust.

Heir: Yes, but that doesn't make you any less determined. Once you adjust you're equally determined, if not more so.

Artist: Yes, yes — but determination can blind you.

Director: Is that because when you're determined, you often don't think?

Artist: Exactly! People think determination is a virtue. But it's just an excuse not to use your mind — to think you know, and not to know.

Heir: But that's ridiculous. Of course determination is a virtue. How many determined people do you know?

Artist: Oh, I know plenty, Heir. Plenty who are determined to live a rotten life.

Heir: You're being too harsh. How do you know the rottenness they embrace isn't better than the rottenness they'd otherwise have?

Director: Between the two of you determination doesn't sound so good!

Heir: Then you tell us what would make it good.

Director: Determination is good when you know, and you pursue what you know.

Artist: Ha! People almost always think they know.

Heir: If they don't know, how can we help them?

Artist: By showing them they don't know.

Director: And if we do that, will they then be determined to know?

Artist: Some will. But many will just give up.

Heir: Why? Because knowledge takes courage and is hard to achieve?

Artist: Partly. But mostly it's because they sense it'll take a long time.

~ Ruthlessness (Artist, Director, Heir)

Heir: Here's something I wonder. When you're determined, are you ruthless?

Director: Well, I suppose some of the determined are ruthless.

Heir: Do you think that's good?

Artist: The question isn't whether it's good. It's when it's good.

Heir: So when is it good?

Artist: It's so obvious I can't believe you don't see it!

Heir: Humor me.

Artist: It's good when the people you're ruthless toward don't deserve pity or compassion.

Heir: And when don't people deserve pity or compassion?

Artist: When they've amply demonstrated they have no pity or compassion for you!

Heir: But I don't want people to pity me.

Artist: Not even if you were down on your luck?

Heir: No.

Artist: Then you're the exception.

Director: Oh, come on. Who really wants, actually wants, to be the object of pity?

Heir: Someone who's sick.

Director: Then does the opposite hold? Do the healthy prefer to be dealt with ruthlessly?

Artist: Ha! He's either teasing us or making a very good point.

Heir: What point? We're missing the point. It's bad to be ruthless.

Artist: Heir, Heir. But is it unwise? For someone like you? What leader doesn't need to be ruthless at times?

Heir: Yes, leaders must be ruthless at times. But do they have to think that's good?

~ Mercy (Director, Heir, Sage)

Heir: Why do you think they call mercy sweet?

Sage: Because of its opposite.

Heir: Cruelty?

Sage: Yes. Cruelty is bitter.

Heir: I agree. But is there an intermediate state? In other words, is the absence of mercy always cruel?

Sage: If you're hoping for mercy, and you don't get it, you tell me.

Heir: Fair enough, I suppose. But tell us, Sage. In general, are the wise more merciful or cruel?

Sage: When it comes to leaders? In their public lives? It all depends.

Heir: On what?

Sage: On what, in the absence of passion, they determine is best.

Director: Sage, are you saying a wise leader must act according to reason and only to reason?

Sage: That's the only way.

Heir: So if reason says it's good policy to be merciful, the wise leader is merciful? And if reason says it's good policy to be cruel, the wise leader is cruel?

Sage: Yes.

Heir: Director?

Director: Sage seems to be making sense. But I'd ask: When is it good policy to be cruel?

Sage: When mercy will undermine the leader's cause.

Heir: But what kind of cause is it if it takes being cruel?

Sage: The kind that often carries the day.

~ Cruelty (Artist, Director, Heir, Sage)

Heir: Well, I intend to carry the day through being kind.

Sage: Still, you'd better be prepared to be cruel.

Heir: Why?

Sage: Look at it this way. If you act out of kindness ninety-nine times, and then the one-hundredth time it's clear you need to be cruel — what happens if you fail to be cruel?

Heir: It's really clear? Alright, I'll concede the point. Let's say it's clear. I don't know what happens if I fail to be cruel.

Artist: I do. You jeopardize the ninety-nine.

Sage: Yes. You put everything at risk.

Heir: What? And that's why we're cruel? Because everything is at risk?

Sage: That's when it makes sense to be cruel.

Heir: But can't I try to kill with kindness, as they say?

Sage: Sometimes you have to act right away with no time to waste in hoping kindness will bring things around.

Director: Yes, Sage. But what puts the ninety-nine at risk? That's something I don't understand.

Sage: The fruits of kindness are fragile, Director.

Director: The fruits? I'm afraid I still don't understand.

Sage: Tell me. Is kindness from a leader for its own sake, or is it for something else?

Director: From a leader? I'd say it's for both.

Sage: Well, the one-hundredth time in our example involves an attack on the 'something else'.

Heir: But, Sage, if there were no 'something else', there'd be no need to be cruel?

Sage: That's right. But if there were no 'something else' you wouldn't be a true leader. You'd be a kind-hearted fool.

~ Urbanity (Director, Sage)

Sage: Do you think I was too blunt with Heir?

Director: I wouldn't worry. But tell me. How important is urbanity to your practice?

Sage: Oh, it's crucial. I have to keep things smooth so no one takes offense at my advice.

Director: Do people often take offense?

Sage: Ha, ha. You're basically asking if I'm truly urbane.

Director: Well, yes. But aren't there times when you have to push a bit?

Sage: Yes, of course. But how is it with you and philosophy?

Director: You mean do I offend?

Sage: Yes.

Director: At times.

Sage: It just can't be helped?

Director: Oh, it can be helped.

Sage: But you choose not to help? Why?

Director: Because that's sometimes what it takes to see something more clearly.

Sage: But can't you just show them gently?

Director: I'm usually the one trying to see.

Sage: See what?

Director: Something about the person I'm talking to.

Sage: But what?

Director: How open they are to philosophy.

Sage: And how open do you find me?

Director: Ah, Sage. A straight answer to that would be less than urbane.

~ Sophistication (Director, Heir)

Director: This is quite a crowd you have here, Heir.

Heir: Yes, and a sophisticated one at that.

Director: What does it mean to be sophisticated?

Heir: It means you're aware of and able to interpret complex issues.

Director: But doesn't it also mean you have a great deal of experience?

Heir: Yes, of course. That's how you know how to deal with complex issues.

Director: What makes an issue complex?

Heir: Isn't it obvious?

Director: Not always. But I think issues often become complex when different cultures are involved.

Heir: Well, if you have experience in the cultures, you can figure things out.

Director: And you get this experience by traveling abroad?

Heir: Not necessarily. We have many different cultures here in our own nation.

Director: Hmm. I wonder if you and I have the same idea of culture. What's yours?

Heir: Culture is a way of doing things, of living.

Director: And if that's what a culture is, then a culture can involve a great many people or very few. No?

Heir: Of course. Even a family, for instance, can have a culture of its own. But what's your idea?

Director: I prefer to say a culture is a way of understanding.

Heir: Interesting. But can we ever truly understand another's way of understanding?

Director: We can certainly try. But what if we try to understand something as complex as a nation, with millions of families and other sorts of cultural groups?

Heir: And we hope to understand enough to do justice to each? That's simple. We can't.

~ Simplicity (Artist, Director, Heir)

Artist: You have to have a simple message.

Director: One that everyone can understand?

Artist: Yes.

Director: So you speak to the lowest common denominator?

Artist: Of course.

Director: Heir, is there a single common denominator across your constituency?

Heir: Well, we're all human.

Director: Yes, but aren't we all human in different ways? What about the cultures we were just talking about? Do they all have something in common?

Heir: The important things, yes.

Director: Really? So their differences are merely superficial?

Heir: I wouldn't say that.

Director: So they have important differences?

Heir: They do.

Director: Differences that don't reduce to a common denominator?

Artist: What are you suggesting, Director? That he needs a sophisticated message that speaks to them all? That never works. Half the battle is deciding who you're speaking to, and making it very simple for them.

Director: Well, numbers are what count. Right?

Heir: Of course.

Director: And you want to win. Yes?

Heir: You know I do.

Director: Then speak simply to the denominator that has the most votes. And speak to the others once you're in.

~ Flexible (Artist, Director)

Artist: Speak to the others once you're in? Ha!

Director: What's wrong, Artist?

Artist: What will he have to say?

Director: Well, truth be told, I suppose he'll mostly listen.

Artist: And what is it he'll listen to?

Director: Their needs.

Artist: Exactly the problem!

Director: Why?

Artist: Because he can't fulfill them!

Director: Because?

Artist: Because he has to look out for the denominator that has the most votes! That's what got him in!

Director: Yes, Artist, but once he's in won't he have some flexibility?

Artist: Yes, sure. But if he's too flexible do you know what happens?

Director: He won't get elected again.

Artist: Precisely!

Director: So he can be somewhat flexible. That's better than nothing, no?

Artist: Yes, yes — it's better than nothing.

Director: You know, I sometimes wonder why more officials aren't more flexible.

Artist: At best it's because they don't command enough support to afford the luxury.

Director: But Heir will have that support. Won't he?

Artist: True. So what are you saying? He'll squander his political capital on flexibility?

Director: Knowing him? He'll find a way to turn flexibility into a capital of its own.

~ Independence (Director, Heir, Sage)

Director: How can leaders be independent?

Sage: That's the ultimate problem.

Director: Why?

Sage: Because they serve.

Heir: Oh, but everyone serves in one way or another. It's how we serve that makes us independent or not.

Director: How should we serve?

Heir: With dignity.

Director: Dignity makes us independent?

Heir: I wouldn't say it makes us independent. I'd say it's a sign of independence.

Director: But then what is it that makes us independent?

Heir: Living up to certain standards.

Director: Which standards?

Heir: The standards that.... The standards....

Sage: The standards we choose for ourselves.

Heir: Yes, thank you.

Director: How do we know what to choose?

Heir: Director, you're just being impossible now.

Director: Am I? What's wrong with asking a few questions about something as important as 'the ultimate problem'?

Heir: We choose high standards. That's what makes us independent.

Director: And will any old high standards do? Or do we need the right ones for the job?

Heir: We need the right ones. And I know what you'll ask: How do we know which ones are right? Well, leaders know this instinctively. If they don't — they're not fit to lead.

~ Character (Director, Heir, Sage)

Sage: I think we may have been going about this all wrong. We should have been talking about character.

Director: Character will get you elected?

Sage: Not character alone. But it's a big help.

Director: I take it you're talking about good character.

Sage: Yes, of course.

Director: And a good character would never, for instance, steal.

Sage: Of course not.

Director: Not even from an enemy during war?

Sage: Well, war is different.

Director: How?

Sage: The enemy wouldn't hesitate to steal from you.

Director: So the principle is that it's fine to steal from those who would steal from you?

Heir: So what are you saying, Director? That a good leader steals from thieves?

Director: I'm not trying to say anything, Heir. I'm just trying to understand what a good character would or wouldn't do. And you should, too, if it will help you get elected.

Heir: You don't think I have a good character?

Director: I did — until it became a question of election.

Heir: Why do you say that?

Director: Because elections can be an ugly business, and good characters don't engage in ugly business. Do they?

Heir: The key is that elections 'can be' ugly. My campaign won't be like that.

Director: But what if the other side gets ugly?

Heir: Then they've declared war.

- Reputation (Artist, Director)

Artist: We need to talk to Heir about his reputation.

Director: Why?

Artist: He can get a little wild at times.

Director: Then shouldn't the voters know that about him?

Artist: It will hurt his chances!

Director: Then maybe he shouldn't be elected.

Artist: Now I know you're not being serious.

Director: You'd have him project a false image of himself?

Artist: No, but he doesn't need to shoot himself in the foot.

Director: And he avoids that by portraying himself as somewhat other than he is?

Artist: Look, reputation isn't always a perfectly snug fit with truth. It's a little flexible.

Director: If you go into battle, do you want a spear that's flexible or firm?

Artist: Yes, yes. Of course you want the firm spear — though maybe with a little give.

Director: Then we should talk to Heir mostly about his behavior, not his reputation.

Artist: I don't know, Director. His behavior is part of who he is.

Director: You're saying we have to take the bad with the good?

Artist: Yes.

Director: And his good outweighs his bad?

Artist: By a far cry, yes.

Director: And his good outweighs the good of his opponent?

Artist: I have no doubt about that. And I know you don't either.

Director: Then what can we do to help him win?

Artist: Talk to him — about his reputation!

~ Roles (Artist, Director, Heir)

Artist: Now, when you're in one role, certain things are expected of you. And when you're in another role, other things are expected.

Heir: And let me guess. When you're running for office, people expect that you won't run wild.

Artist: Yes! I mean, yes. And isn't it good to live up to people's expectations when you're asking for their vote?

Heir: Of course it is.

Director: But is it?

Heir: Here we go again. What now?

Director: What if people have unreasonable expectations?

Heir: People always have unreasonable expectations.

Director: Then why try to live up to them? Or do you think you should only pretend to live up to them?

Heir: That's what most politicians do. Isn't it?

Director: I don't know. I'd have to talk to them to find out.

Heir: But here you are talking to me.

Director: Do you want to live up to unreasonable expectations?

Heir: I can tell you definitely — no.

Director: And you don't want to fool the electorate?

Heir: I don't.

Artist: Then what do you want to do?

Heir: Play the role of a teacher.

Artist: A teacher? Ha! You'd teach the electorate what's reasonable?

Heir: Yes. And I'm counting on the two of you to help me do just that.

~ Eccentricity (Artist, Director, Heir)

Heir: I think the wise are often eccentric.

Artist: Yes, and there's nothing more eccentric than trying to teach the electorate. But I'm not saying that makes you wise.

Heir: But be honest, now. Don't you find the eccentric refreshing? Director?

Director: Yes, I know what you mean. There's something charming about the unconventional and slightly strange. Take Artist, for instance.

Artist: Take yourself.

Heir: You don't think you're somewhat eccentric?

Artist: I sometimes think I'm more crazy than eccentric.

Heir: Why would you say that?

Artist: What's more sure a sign of genius? Eccentricity or madness?

Heir: Who can say? But when I think of artistic genius, I surely think of you!

Director: I see you're careful to limit Artist to artistic genius.

Artist: You don't think artistic genius is the summit of all genius?

Director: If I think of it as a summit, I think of it as part of a twin peak.

Heir: What's the other peak?

Director: Political genius.

Heir: But what about philosophy? There's no third peak?

Director: No, there isn't.

Heir: Then is philosophy part artistic and part political?

Director: That's a very good question, Heir. And the answer is no.

Heir: But surely there's a philosophical genius.

Director: Maybe. But if there is, it spends its time not in being a peak but in exploring the peaks. And between the two of you, there's plenty for philosophy to do.

- Confidence (Heir, Sage)

Heir: Do you think I'm odd?

Sage: I'd say you're unusual.

Heir: In a good way?

Sage: Of course in a good way.

Heir: What's unusual about me?

Sage: You're a strange blend of things.

Heir: What things come most to mind?

Sage: You're a blend of confidence and doubt.

Heir: Aren't we all a blend of confidence and doubt?

Sage: Yes, but you take it to extremes.

Heir: How so?

Sage: On the one hand you're ready to take on the world. On the other hand I sometimes feel the sight of your own shadow might knock you out of the race.

Heir: Shadows are frightening things.

Sage: Then I'd say you're at your best right at high noon.

Heir: Or during the night.

Sage: True.

Heir: But tell me what high noon means.

Sage: In my metaphor? It means the height of the crisis, the greatest tension.

Heir: Yes, I'm usually comfortable with that.

Sage: And that's what makes you seem odd. It's almost as though you're not even aware of the crisis. Some might think there's something wrong with you. But I know it's just the opposite. Dealing with crises comes naturally to you.

Heir: Yes. And so long as there's plenty of trouble — I deserve to win.

- Inclusiveness (Artist, Director, Heir)

Heir: I want to include as many of the people as I can when I take office.

Director: You mean you want them to help you with your work?

Heir: Yes. And doesn't that seem wise?

Artist: What's wise about that?

Heir: It's how I'll get elected to a second term. They'll all campaign for me.

Artist: But who do you think will be willing to help? Successful people?

Heir: Why not?

Artist: Because they're too busy with their own affairs to help you with yours.

Heir: But what if I make their business my business?

Artist: Yes, yes — but what if they tell you to mind your own business?

Heir: So you think only the unsuccessful will want to be included in my work? Well, I'll tell you something. Many of the 'unsuccessful' are unsuccessful simply because they haven't been given their proper task.

Artist: And you know what that task is?

Heir: When it comes to serving my cause? Always. So have no doubt.

Director: Yes, but will you blame these people if your cause starts to fail?

Heir: I'd only blame myself.

Director: Because you're the leader?

Heir: Right. And because blaming others is weak.

Director: So how do you avoid failure?

Artist: I'll tell you one way. You cull the weak from the team.

Director: Even if they're volunteers?

Artist: Oh, there's nothing sacred about volunteers. Drop them if they're no good. And with any luck they'll go work for the enemy — and threaten their cause instead.

~ Exclusiveness (Director, Sage)

Sage: Heir needs to learn how to exclude.

Director: Why do you say that?

Sage: He looks at life as one giant party to which everyone is invited.

Director: He does like his parties. But who do you think he needs to exclude?

Sage: Those who want to take advantage of him.

Director: How would they take advantage of him?

Sage: Isn't it obvious?

Director: Not to me.

Sage: Well, they'd leech onto him.

Director: And what blood would they suck? His money?

Sage: No, not his money.

Director: What then?

Sage: His influence.

Director: You can steal someone's influence?

Sage: Of course you can. You enlist them to your cause, whatever it might be.

Director: Ah, I think I see. Too many causes and Heir is all used up.

Sage: Exactly. So he needs to be careful.

Director: What's your cause, Sage?

Sage: As far as Heir is concerned? Why, it's Heir himself. What's yours?

Director: Heir himself, but Heir as tempered by philosophy.

Sage: Well, mine is Heir as tempered by wisdom.

Director: Can we make common cause?

Sage: So long as philosophy remains the love of wisdom? Of course we can.

~ Science (Director, Heir, Sage)

Heir: Look at that sunset! This is my favorite time of day.

Sage: Are you sure your favorite time isn't noon?

Heir: Noon and night. And sunset leads me into the night!

Director: The night of the mind?

Heir: Ha, ha. No, of course not. The mind shines bright even in total darkness.

Director: Because of science?

Heir: Well, that's an interesting question. What do you think science is?

Director: Something much more than test tubes and the like.

Heir: You're thinking of science in a very broad sense?

Director: The broadest possible sense. Science is the proper functioning of the mind.

Sage: And when does the mind function properly?

Director: When it never turns off.

Heir: When does the mind turn off?

Director: Whenever it comes across something and says, 'That's not a matter for thought.'

Heir: I agree. And then its lights go out.

Sage: So, in other words, you're saying science is, essentially, a matter of being on or awake?

Director: Yes, in so many words.

Sage: That's a strange definition of science, Director.

Director: If you want an even stranger definition, ask me what politics is.

Sage: I will. But I know politics and science don't always mix.

Director: They don't. And that's why we're all counting on Heir — to keep stirring things up.

~ People (Artist, Director, Heir, Sage)

Artist: Will you treat everyone as an individual? Or will you treat everyone as a people? Do you know what I'm asking?

Heir: Of course I do. I think there's a time for each.

Director: When do you treat people as people and not individuals?

Heir: When dealing with the common interest.

Director: And you treat people as individuals when dealing with individual interests?

Heir: Yes.

Artist: But who has time for individual interests?

Heir: I will.

Director: What happens when those you've treated as people learn that you've treated others as individuals?

Heir: You're asking if they'll resent it?

Director: Yes.

Heir: Well, the real question is, for any of them — did they get what they wanted?

Sage: If I get what I want, I don't care if I'm treated as a people or an individual?

Heir: That's right.

Director: How many individuals do you think you'll have to deal with? In other words, will your time be spent mostly on people or individuals?

Heir: My time will go mostly to people.

Artist: But who do you like better? People or individuals?

Heir: I like them both equally. Who do you three like?

Artist: I like individuals.

Sage: And I like individuals.

Director: And I do, too. So it looks like you're alone.

~ Enlightenment (Director, Sage)

Sage: Do you know what I think Heir will be good for, very good for? The diffusion of knowledge.

Director: You mean he's a proponent of the Enlightenment?

Sage: Yes.

Director: Are you a proponent of the Enlightenment, Sage?

Sage: Of course I am. What makes you ask?

Director: Well, it has to do with your wisdom.

Sage: What do you mean?

Director: Enlightenment brings all wisdom out into the light.

Sage: What's wrong with that?

Director: If all of your wisdom is brought out into the light, what's left for you?

Sage: Ha, ha. You don't think wisdom can be shared with the worthy?

Director: You think it can?

Sage: Of course I do! If I didn't, how would I be of interest to you as a philosopher?

Director: But that's precisely why you'd be of interest to me.

Sage: I don't understand.

Director: I want to reach in and pluck out all the wisdom that's hidden.

Sage: Have you ever had success in that?

Director: Just because I'm not very good at what I attempt doesn't mean the attempt isn't worthwhile.

Sage: That's true. But what about your wisdom, your own private wisdom? Why don't you share that?

Director: Oh, I do! But then I often find I'm not as wise as I sometimes suppose myself to be.

~ Strategy (Artist, Director)

Artist: How can we help Heir with his strategy?

Director: Strategy to win or strategy to govern?

Artist: Shouldn't they be the same?

Director: You might have a point.

Artist: Yes, but you might have a point, too.

Director: If I have a point, what is it?

Artist: Ha! I'll tell you what it is. The electorate always has an idea of what it takes to win, but it often has no idea what it takes to govern. So the strategies must differ.

Director: And does it go like this? In my campaign I promise ABC, a winning promise. And people assume it takes DEF to accomplish that. But I know it actually takes XYZ. So when I win, I set out for XYZ, deliver ABC, and let the people think what they will?

Artist: Yes.

Director: Do you think Heir is up for that?

Artist: Positively.

Director: But he wants to be inclusive.

Artist: You mean people will see the XYZ?

Director: Yes. Will that be a problem?

Artist: Maybe he's only inclusive up to a point.

Director: The point just before where things actually get done?

Artist: Yes. What do you think?

Director: I'm not sure people would settle for that.

Artist: Oh, they'll settle if they get their ABC.

Director: But if they don't settle?

Artist: Then politics will have been stood on its head.

~ Tactics (Director, Heir)

Heir: People think wisdom is in the strategy. And there's some truth to that. But the real wisdom shines in the tactics.

Director: Wisdom in the tactics? How so?

Heir: Strategies once set stay more or less set. But tactics constantly change.

Director: And it takes wisdom to change?

Heir: To change for the better? Of course.

Director: But does that mean wisdom itself changes?

Heir: How could that be? Wisdom is wisdom.

Director: Hmm. When does wisdom bring about a change in tactics?

Heir: When circumstances change.

Director: And when they change, and the tactics change, can the strategy still be sound?

Heir: Yes. But if the circumstances change to a great enough degree, then the tactics too must change to a great degree. And when that happens, the strategy itself must change — or strategy and tactics will be out of sync.

Director: But why can't strategy drive the change in tactics? I mean, if circumstances change to a great degree, can't strategy take the lead?

Heir: Of course. But what do you think is more sensitive to change? Strategy or tactics?

Director: Well, tactics are on the ground, as they say.

Heir: Yes. They see things first. And would you have them wait for strategy to awaken to what's going on?

Director: But what does it take to awaken strategy?

Heir: Often enough? A change in tactics. And strategy hates waking to this, because it likes to feel it's in control.

Director: Well, I think there's some truth to that. But it makes me wonder what all this means for politics — and philosophy, too.

- Emulation (Artist, Director, Heir)

Heir: Who would I emulate? No one.

Artist: You don't look to anyone for inspiration, as an example of what can be done?

Heir: Oh, yes. Of course I do. But I'm not looking to imitate anyone.

Artist: Not even if in doing so you surpass them?

Heir: The only one I want to surpass is myself.

Director: And how do you surpass yourself?

Heir: I keep on getting better and better.

Director: So, Heir, if you win this election you'll get better by winning an even greater election?

Heir: No, that's not what I mean.

Director: Then what do you mean?

Heir: I'll improve as a person.

Director: You'll become a better person?

Heir: Yes.

Director: Better at what? Winning elections and governing?

Heir: Why are you giving me a hard time?

Director: If you think this is a hard time, what will you think while on campaign?

Heir: Yes, but I expect you to support me.

Director: Support you by leaving you so you can't support yourself when pressed?

Heir: Ha. Well, now I know who I want to emulate.

Director: Who?

Heir: You! I'm going to press my electorate.

Artist: Ha! Good luck with that. You're not Director. And they're not you.

- Fruits (Artist, Director, Heir, Sage)

Director: So tell us, Heir. What will be the fruits of your time in office?

Heir: Greater prosperity, greater harmony — things like that.

Artist: But won't your opponent claim to bring greater prosperity and harmony, too?

Heir: Yes. But I can really do it.

Sage: How?

Heir: By getting people to talk, to make connections with one another.

Director: I can see how that might lead to greater harmony, but how does it lead to greater prosperity?

Heir: Prosperity requires that intelligent deals be made. You can't have intelligent deals without honest talk and the right connections.

Director: How will you encourage people to be honest?

Heir: By being honest myself.

Director: Honest about what? How important it is to be honest?

Heir: I'll be honest about everything I can be honest about.

Director: Then you'd expect the same of those you govern? They'll be honest about what they can be honest about, too?

Heir: Yes.

Director: And that includes being honest in their intelligent deals?

Heir: Of course. That's the whole point.

Director: Now what about the right connections? What makes a connection right?

Heir: When something good can come of it.

Director: Something like a deal? Or something good like friendship?

Heir: Why not both?

Director: That's fine, as long as we're not afraid to ask, in either case — at what price?

~ Deals (Artist, Director, Heir, Sage)

Sage: What price is too high to pay for harmony, Director?

Director: Harmony? I think that price has to do with honesty, Sage.

Sage: I'm not sure I follow.

Director: What is harmony?

Sage: Agreement.

Director: Can you agree to something you really don't want to agree to?

Sage: Of course.

Director: And then there's harmony?

Sage: There may be a superficial harmony, but not one that's deep and true.

Heir: Then that's the price that's too high. The sacrifice of the deep and true.

Artist: And that's the sacrifice altruists make.

Heir: What do you mean?

Artist: They sacrifice their own feeling of harmony for the sake of someone else's.

Heir: But then it's not a true harmony. I mean, if they're faking, the note they bring to the harmony isn't true. It's dishonest. Do you know what I mean?

Artist: Yes, of course I do.

Heir: So if altruists really care, they'll care about the quality of their own note first. That way they can try to make a true harmony, and not one that has a false ring.

Director: Do you think people can always tell when harmony is false?

Heir: If they're trained in harmony, yes. But many people don't experience much harmony in their lives. And so they don't know the real thing from the fake.

Artist: Oh, I think most people can tell.

Heir: Then why do so many false harmonies exist?

Artist: I suspect it's because the people involved — somehow struck a deal.

- Comfort (Artist, Director, Heir)

Artist: And if you want my opinion, I'll tell you about the nature of that deal.

Heir: Please do.

Artist: It's all about comfort.

Heir: Comfort? But what comfort is there if there's no true harmony?

Artist: Oh, every harmony has its comfort, even the less than true.

Heir: That's ridiculous, Artist. Nothing would make me less comfortable than a false harmony.

Artist: Live without harmony long enough and you might change your tune.

Heir: Never.

Director: Have you ever been very much uncomfortable, Heir?

Heir: Harmony wise?

Director: Is there some other greater discomfort we should be talking about?

Heir: No. But you're asking a rather personal question, don't you think?

Director: Yes, but have you?

Heir: Have you ever been very much uncomfortable, Director?

Director: I'm often uncomfortable.

Heir: Well, so am I. But not because I accept false harmonies.

Director: And you're never tempted to accept them? Why?

Heir: Because I believe in myself.

Director: What does that mean?

Heir: I believe I deserve better.

Director: Well, I'm not sure what I deserve. But I know what I want. And it sounds like we're after just the same thing.

- Purity (Director, Heir)

Heir: So how can we get what we're after?

Director: We have to concentrate.

Heir: On what?

Director: The quality of the notes we hear.

Heir: And only pay attention to those that are pure?

Director: If we're looking for the ones that harmonize with us? Sure. But, I think this is going to be very hard for you.

Heir: Why?

Director: Your political career will force you to deal with most every sort of note you can imagine.

Heir: And most of them won't be pure?

Director: Well, most of them won't be pure and in harmony with you.

Heir: Yes, but back up a step. Do you think most of them won't be pure?

Director: Why does it matter?

Heir: Because I'll have to broker deals. And I would never make one between someone whose note is true and someone whose note is false.

Director: And if the true are few it will be that much harder to match them up?

Heir: Yes. And isn't that what you'd do? Match true with true?

Director: I'm not a politician, so I don't know.

Heir: Do you only think about things that have to do with you?

Director: Isn't that the best way to concentrate? But I'll tell you. I sometimes think about things that have to do with you. And yes, I'd be inclined to match like with like.

Heir: And when they're all matched up and the poor harmonies outnumber the rich?

Director: Then maybe the rich have to find a way to sing all on their own.

~ Endurance (Artist, Heir)

Heir: Artist, how do you keep on putting out work after work?

Artist: I just take one step at a time.

Heir: But we all take one step at a time.

Artist: Yes, but the real answer is that I'm always walking.

Heir: Are you suggesting that in my run for office I should walk?

Artist: Of course not. The trick is endurance. If you can keep up a run, then you should run your race. But if you win you might consider setting your pace at a brisk walk.

Heir: Because I can't keep up the run?

Artist: Actually, I was thinking less about you than others.

Heir: You mean the others won't be able to keep up the run. And so I should walk?

Artist: Yes.

Heir: But why not take it further? Why not say I should set my pace at a leisurely walk?

Artist: Because then too many people will be able to keep up with you.

Heir: What happens then?

Artist: I think you know what happens then. But I'll tell you one thing, Heir. Your enemies keep pace.

Heir: But what if they keep pace even with a brisk walk?

Artist: If they keep pace and endure over time? Consider making them your friends.

Heir: Endurance is that important? But what about who they are as people?

Artist: Oh, of course that's important, too. And who they are might be athletes who can serve your cause.

Heir: So what should I do? Ask them to run ahead and report what they see?

Artist: Exactly so. And do you know what it means if they prove true again and again?

Heir: I'm forced to call them friends.

~ Elegance (Artist, Director, Heir, Sage)

Heir: What I want to be known for most in my campaign? I don't know. I haven't really thought that through. What do you think?

Sage: I think it should be elegance — grace and simplicity.

Heir: Why that?

Sage: It's appealing.

Heir: But shouldn't I aim for something with more... substance?

Sage: Oh, your substance will take care of itself.

Artist: But, Sage, don't you think that's irresponsible? You seem to be suggesting that form is more important than substance.

Sage: Why, no. Both should be as one in a good campaign.

Director: And if as one, that means both substance and form can be elegant? Which means it's possible they can be inelegant, too?

Sage: True.

Director: So what's it like in a bad campaign? The substance is elegant but the form is inelegant?

Sage: Yes. Or the substance is inelegant but the form is elegant.

Director: And how would you describe these campaigns?

Sage: The former is unfortunate, while the latter is a lie.

Heir: And for me, you trust my substance is elegant?

Sage: I know it's elegant.

Heir: So how do I ensure my form is, too?

Sage: Just don't think about the form, and let your substance shine through.

Artist: Ha! You say the substance will take care of itself. And then you say not to worry about the form. So it's a magical sort of campaign! And one I think will fail.

~ Humor (Artist, Director, Heir, Sage)

Heir: I think you three should know that, beyond elegance, there's something I want to be known for.

Sage: What?

Heir: My sense of humor.

Director: Humor is beyond elegance?

Heir: Of course it is! You can have a sense of humor about your elegance, can't you, Director?

Artist: But why would you make fun of that?

Heir: Because elegance can lead to hubris. You need to show people that you don't take yourself too seriously.

Director: But what if you weren't running for office? Would you poke fun at your elegance then?

Heir: Of course I would. I wouldn't want to alienate my friends.

Artist: Oh, Heir. I don't need humor to tolerate your elegance. In fact, I would find humor annoying.

Sage: Why would it be annoying?

Artist: Because it assumes I'm the sort of person who can't appreciate pure elegance. And that's an insult to me.

Director: Do you think humor about elegance insults the electorate?

Artist: Some of them.

Sage: But what counts in elections is most of them, not some of them.

Artist: And that's the problem with elections, Sage.

Director: So do you think Heir shouldn't run?

Artist: No, clearly he should run. It's his way. But that doesn't mean he shouldn't feel free to be privately and seriously — elegant with us.

~ Perspective (Artist, Director, Heir, Sage)

Director: What's the difference between humor and perspective?

Heir: I'll tell you. Not much. You need perspective in order to have humor. And you can just as easily say you need humor in order to have perspective.

Director: Then humor and perspective seem equally important.

Artist: Yes, yes. But there's an important sort of humor that doesn't necessarily involve perspective. Mockery.

Sage: Your favorite type.

Director: What happens if you're in the habit of mocking everything you see?

Heir: People will distance themselves from you.

Director: Can that distance give you, the mocker, perspective?

Heir: I don't see how it can.

Director: Why not?

Heir: Because mockery isn't really humor. Maybe it would be if it only teased. But mockery contains an element of contempt.

Artist: And humor and contempt are incompatible?

Sage: Of course they are, Artist. I should know. I once mocked.

Director: But you no longer do? Why?

Sage: Because I wanted more honesty.

Artist: Honesty? Ha! You don't think you can be honest when you're mocking for all you're worth?

Sage: You might be honest in a narrow, unreflective sense. But that's precisely why you should stop.

Director: Because you should be honest in a broad, reflective sense?

Sage: Yes. And when you are, you'll find — that humor and perspective are one.

~ Dissembling (Director, Heir)

Heir: It's almost never good to dissemble to the electorate.

Director: 'Almost', Heir?

Heir: There are times when a leader must.

Director: When?

Heir: Oh, I think it's simple. Here's an example. You work very hard in hopes of signing a treaty for ABCDE. But you only get ABCD. You really wanted E. But you have to put a brave and cheery face on ABCD for the electorate. That's dissembling, and there's nothing wrong with that.

Director: But why is there nothing wrong with that? Why not share your disappointment?

Heir: Because you want people to think you met with success.

Director: But you did. You got A, B, C, and D.

Heir: But my enemies will attack the lack of E.

Director: Can't you just let them attack and let people decide for themselves how successful you were?

Heir: You need to teach the people how successful you were.

Director: Why?

Heir: Because otherwise how would they know?

Director: And you'll teach them by dissembling how you feel?

Heir: You think honest feelings are the way for a politician to teach?

Director: Why not? It's never been done before. Maybe it's worth a try.

Heir: Now you're being ridiculous.

Director: More ridiculous than pretending to be happy when you're not?

Heir: Well, you have a point. But what if I'm often unhappy?

Director: Then I'd say you're in the wrong line of work.

~ Diet (Director, Sage)

Sage: I think diet will be very important to Heir in the months to come.

Director: Why do you say that, Sage?

Sage: Because he'll need to be at the peak of his strength.

Director: So he'll need vitamins and minerals?

Sage: Yes, of course. He'll need to eat nutritious things.

Director: And isn't eating the right amount of the right thing key? I mean, if he eats too little he'll be edgy and short. But if he eats too much he'll be dopey and lethargic. No?

Sage: Yes, it's only too true.

Director: But now I wonder about diet in another sense.

Sage: Oh? What sense?

Director: What he reads.

Sage: Reading too little will make him edgy and too much lethargic?

Director: For some of us that's true, no? But the point is that he'll need inspiration.

Sage: So he'll read biographies of others who've had success.

Director: I don't know.

Sage: Why not?

Director: I think Heir wants more success than those who've had success.

Sage: That's unwise, don't you think?

Director: It might be. But I'll tell you what I think he needs. Philosophy.

Sage: How will philosophy help?

Director: It will cut through the nonsense and help him focus on what's real.

Sage: And if he goes hungry on what's real?

Director: Then he doesn't deserve to lead.

~ Reading (Artist, Director, Heir, Sage)

Heir: Reading? Ha, ha. Who has time to read?

Director: Can't you spare half an hour a day to read, and read slowly?

Heir: And what gain is there in that? It'll take me a year to finish a book!

Director: Weren't we just talking about the importance of perspective?

Heir: Yes, but I need my own perspective, not the perspective of some long-dead philosopher.

Artist: Then Director and I will write you something to read.

Director: We will?

Artist: Yes. Director and I will talk, and I'll write up what we said — then give it to you.

Heir: But I can just talk to the two of you. Why would I read what you wrote?

Artist: Because you can say more in writing than you can in person.

Director: You can?

Artist: Of course you can! You're more free.

Heir: But your freedom won't matter if I don't have the time.

Artist: Then we'll have to get your attention so you make the time.

Heir: But what if I'm simply too tired, no matter how much of my attention you get?

Artist: Then you'll make time to read when you're not too tired.

Heir: But I need that time for my campaign!

Sage: Artist, let me see if I can help. When you're playing chess, Heir, is it wise to make a move quickly before you've thought it all the way through?

Heir: No, of course not.

Sage: Well, Artist and Director will write about your possible moves, to help you think things through. And I'll join them in their work — because, as you may have guessed, I know a thing or two about chess.

- Writing (Artist, Director)

Director: So you're going to write up what we discuss and give it to Heir?

Artist: Yes.

Director: What shall we talk about first?

Artist: Writing itself.

Director: Why does Heir need to know about that?

Artist: His office is going to have to produce a great number of documents.

Director: True. So what's important to know about writing?

Artist: That people tend to write in the manner in which they read.

Director: So careless readers make for careless writers?

Artist: Yes, it can't be helped.

Director: And careful readers make for careful writers? But what kind of reader is Heir?

Artist: When he reads? He's an excellent reader.

Director: So when he writes he's an excellent writer, too?

Artist: Yes, but if he doesn't have time to read, how will he have time to write?

Director: Hmm. Then what will he do?

Artist: He'll let others do the reading and writing for him.

Director: How can he get away with that?

Artist: He'll have them give him oral reports on what they've written or read. And then he'll question them thoroughly.

Director: Well then, he'll need a great deal of trust in the abilities of those who report. And an even greater trust in his ability to question effectively. But if that's his way, let's forget about writing something down. Let's talk some more and give him an oral report on what we say. And once we've made that report, and he starts to question us, we'll make use of the privilege of friendship — and question him right back.

~ Renown (Artist, Director, Heir, Sage)

Director: Can you lead without renown?

Heir: Of course not.

Director: Why not?

Heir: Because if people don't know who you are, you'll never be elected.

Director: But once you're elected?

Heir: You're asking if you can lead if people forget about you?

Director: Yes. I'm asking if you can lead quietly.

Heir: I suppose it's possible.

Director: So which is better? Quietly or with noise?

Heir: Well, when you say 'noise'....

Director: What's a better way to put it?

Heir: I'm not sure there is a better way to put it.

Director: Then which is it?

Heir: I'm in favor of a combination of the two.

Artist: Ha! And when will you be which?

Heir: For the things that require great public backing, I'll make noise. But for things that require tactful dealing, I'll keep quiet.

Sage: What sorts of things require tactful dealing, Heir?

Heir: The sorts of things the public wouldn't understand.

Sage: Why wouldn't they understand?

Heir: Because they're not privy to everything that goes on.

Director: What if you made them privy?

Heir: All my peers would turn on me — and I would stand alone.

~ Crowds (Artist, Director, Heir, Sage)

Heir: There's nothing like rousing a crowd.

Director: How does it make you feel?

Heir: Like the crowd feels. Electrified.

Director: Does it matter who's in the crowd?

Heir: What do you mean?

Director: I mean, what if you rouse a crowd from an enemy camp?

Heir: That would be amazing!

Director: Why?

Heir: Because then they'd be on my side.

Sage: Do you think there's a kind of crowd you wouldn't be able to rouse?

Heir: Well, Sage, I don't want to sound arrogant. But no.

Sage: Then let me ask you this. What if you met with each individual from the crowd?

Heir: One by one?

Sage: Yes. Would you be able to win them over?

Heir: I think so.

Sage: But then what if you took everything you said to the individuals and wrapped it all up into a presentation for the reassembled crowd? Would it be coherent?

Heir: You're asking if I'd say different things to different people when meeting one on one? I'd have to make a point not to.

Sage: But then would you be able to win everyone over?

Heir: No, probably not everyone.

Artist: Ha! Of course not everyone! But can you be content with less than all?

Heir: With a mere majority, you mean? Look at it this way. A roaring crowd isn't a majority. It's a force. And that force is what I need.

~ Discretion (Director, Heir)

Director: Discretion is a funny word.

Heir: How so?

Director: On the one hand it involves not offending or revealing private information. On the other hand it involves the freedom to decide what should be done.

Heir: Yes, that is funny. And it's even funnier if you consider that you might have to exercise your discretion to show less than discretion.

Director: When do you imagine you might have to do that?

Heir: When addressing the people.

Director: You'd offend the people?

Heir: Oh, not the people as a whole. But I might offend one or a handful of them.

Director: And what about revealing private information?

Heir: Suppose there are those who privately conspire against the people. Wouldn't it be perfectly within my rights to reveal the conspiracy?

Director: Yes, you have a point. But tell me, Heir. Can you expect discretion from the people?

Heir: Now that's an interesting question. I've never considered that before. I suppose discretion makes no sense when it comes to the people. Who can the people offend? What private information can they reveal?

Director: Hmm. But what about discretion in the other sense?

Heir: Well, it's in their discretion to elect me to office.

Director: But once you're in, during your term?

Heir: Their discretion is considerably less, if almost nonexistent — provided I don't care about being re-elected.

Director: Do you think that's how it ought to be?

Heir: Should the people have more power? I don't know. But as long as I lead, why would I care?

~ Orthodoxy (Artist, Director, Heir, Sage)

Artist: I think you're going to run into trouble.

Heir: Oh?

Artist: There's a certain political orthodoxy you can't offend.

Heir: Can't?

Sage: He's saying it wouldn't be wise.

Heir: But how do we know that?

Sage: What do you mean?

Heir: I know there's an orthodoxy. But who supports it?

Sage: The people.

Heir: Do they? I'd like to find that out.

Director: How would you find that out, Heir?

Heir: I'll ask them.

Artist: And if they say, 'No, we don't believe in the orthodoxy'?

Heir: Then I'm free to ignore it.

Sage: Yes, but your peers will still uphold it. No?

Heir: Who cares? I'll have the people on my side. And some of my peers will leave the orthodoxy behind and come over to us.

Director: Where you'll form a new orthodoxy?

Heir: No, of course not.

Artist: What if you have no say in the matter? What if one just forms?

Heir: Not during my life in office it won't. I'll fight it tooth and nail.

Director: So you'd be free to operate however you see fit?

Heir: Exactly. And the crowds will love it that way.

~ Heterodoxy (Artist, Director)

Artist: Well, he's certainly going to be heterodox.

Director: At the least.

Artist: Why am I finding myself more conservative when talking to him than when I'm away from him?

Director: Because you're being protective.

Artist: Sometimes he scares me.

Director: You think the crowds will turn on him?

Artist: If he doesn't believe what they believe, and that becomes clear? Yes.

Director: Why would it have to become clear?

Artist: Because he's proud.

Director: Would you rather have him be humble?

Artist: I'd rather he show good sense.

Director: Don't worry too much, Artist. He's a quick learner. He's bound to take a few tumbles. But he'll get back on his feet.

Artist: He's going to make a lot of enemies, you know.

Director: Yes, he will. But he'll make more and better friends.

Artist: Who'll share his heterodox views?

Director: Some will.

Artist: And the others?

Director: Fellow travelers who'll share an interest or two.

Artist: And they'll be enough to defend him when the time comes for his opponents to demand a declaration of faith?

Director: Maybe not enough. But don't underestimate how broadly attractive an Heir in that kind of trouble can be.

~ Heresy (Artist, Director, Heir, Sage)

Sage: Yes, but there's heterodoxy and then there's heresy.

Director: What's the difference?

Sage: Heterodoxy can be tolerated. Heresy can't.

Heir: So what are you saying? If I show heretical views I won't be elected?

Sage: Of course you won't.

Heir: And if I do manage to get elected, because I showed no heretical views, if I show them while I'm in office, I'll get thrown out?

Sage: Maybe not thrown out but certainly rendered powerless.

Heir: Well, the trick then is not to seem to be heretical.

Artist: But you are heretical!

Director: Artist, you, whose works might well be considered heresy, would accuse another?

Artist: Yes, yes — but we can be, and need to be, honest among friends.

Director: Well, then let me tell you the honest truth. Heresy, strictly speaking, doesn't exist in our country.

Artist: Ha! Just try expressing certain points of view and then tell me it doesn't exist.

Heir: I want to be the defender of those points of view.

Artist: Oh, this is a madhouse! Heir, no crowd will stand behind you if you defend heretical views.

Heir: Then the crowd can't know that's what I do.

Artist: How will it not know?

Heir: I'll lend quiet support. And the ones I support will exercise discretion.

Sage: Wouldn't it be easier, and safer, just to steer well clear?

Heir: It would. But then how am I a champion of freedom?

- One (Director, Heir)

Heir: Artist doesn't have to worry about me. I'm not stupid, you know.

Director: I know you're not. So does Artist. But I am a bit surprised at how worried he is.

Heir: If I were as cautious as he wants me to be — I wouldn't be me!

Director: And that's the only thing you should be cautious about.

Heir: Cautious about always being me? Yes, I agree.

Director: And how will you always be you?

Heir: By always doing what I think I should do.

Director: So you always think before acting? What does it mean to think?

Heir: To weigh and to judge.

Director: And you can judge when it's politically safe to offer your opinion? Because you've weighed the likely response? But what about when you're with crowds? You said you get electrified. And when you're electrified isn't there a risk you'll get carried away?

Heir: Not at all. I can sense when I'm with the crowd and when I'm not. I know the political. And the crowd is the political in its raw form. So when I'm one with the crowd, it's on.

Director: You mean that's when you're really you? But are you a crowd? Do you know what I'm asking?

Heir: I do. And now I see you want to caution me. So let me tell you — I'm no crowd.

Director: But if you're at one with something, aren't you that thing?

Heir: I've heard you talk about being at one with philosophy. Are you philosophy?

Director: When we're at one? I am. And Artist is art. And Sage is wisdom, when he's at one with wisdom. But poor old you — you're just a crowd.

Heir: Conductors aren't the orchestra, and yet they can be at one with the players.

Director: Yes, and together they make music. What do you and your crowd make?

Heir: That remains to be seen.

~ Daring (Artist, Director, Sage)

Sage: I don't know that people are looking for daring in their politicians.

Director: But do you think they're looking for daring in their leaders?

Artist: You have a point, Director. Yes, we do want daring in a leader, a true leader. But we don't seem to want it in the average politician.

Director: Don't you have to earn the title 'leader'? I mean, all you have to do to be a politician is be elected. But leadership takes something more. No?

Artist: It's the daring. Successful daring lifts you out of the mass of politicians and establishes you as a leader.

Sage: There's some truth to that. But this successful daring can't be any old daring. It must be daring backed by wisdom.

Artist: And what does wisdom do for daring?

Sage: It ensures it's nicely planned.

Artist: You mean it should look like daring but it's really not?

Sage: No. I mean it's been thought through.

Director: But can't all politicians think things through?

Sage: Well....

Artist: Yes, and that's the problem. Politicians count their votes. That's how they 'think'. But leaders dare to fight the odds.

Director: But how can you get anything done in a legislature if you always fight the odds?

Sage: I don't see how. Legislatures vote.

Artist: Then maybe it's not about getting things done in the legislature. Maybe it's about daring to tell the truth.

Sage: But you don't have to be elected to tell the truth.

Director: And you don't have to be elected to lead.

~ Points of View (Artist, Director)

Artist: If you're going to tell the truth, you need to know how to say it.

Director: In what sense?

Artist: Suppose you're speaking about things of extreme importance, things of the utmost gravity. How should you speak?

Director: Let me guess. The weight of the speech should match the weight of the subject.

Artist: Yes. Matters of gravity should be spoken of with gravity.

Director: Well, that only seems wise. And if you're dealing with light things you should speak lightly?

Artist: Of course. People will think you're a fool if you speak about light things heavily. Just as they'll think you're a fool for speaking about heavy things lightly.

Director: On which side do philosophers tend to err?

Artist: Both! Light things heavily and heavy things lightly.

Director: Why do you think that is?

Artist: They're always trying to get people to see things from a new perspective.

Director: And do people think they're fools?

Artist: Mostly. But sometimes they succeed and people adopt their point of view.

Director: But I would have thought you'd say philosophers encourage people to develop their own point of view.

Artist: Well, there are philosophers and then there are philosophers.

Director: Just as there are different types of artists?

Artist: Just so.

Director: And what about leaders?

Artist: Leaders? Ha! Leaders all want people to see things their way, the leader's way. But they're limited — by how much they have to see things the way their followers do.

~ Imagination (Heir, Sage)

Heir: Do the wise use their imagination more than other people?

Sage: Yes, certainly.

Heir: How so?

Sage: The wise imagine all the possibilities.

Heir: What does that mean?

Sage: They envision all the possible consequences of a course of action.

Heir: But why do they merely envision or imagine? Why don't they know?

Sage: Oh, they can know what's likely. But knowing something is likely isn't the same as feeling what it'll be like.

Heir: And you use your imagination for that?

Sage: Yes.

Heir: But what if your imagination runs wild? Isn't that worse than not imagining at all?

Sage: Well, if we're talking about running wild....

Heir: Yes. If it runs wild, you'll go to extremes. You might imagine a course of action will make you feel incredibly good. You might imagine a course of action will make you feel incredibly bad.

Sage: And the former will make you foolhardy and the latter overly cautious?

Heir: Right.

Sage: So what do you suggest we do?

Heir: Greatly limit the use of our imagination. Decide what to do based on knowledge.

Sage: Without insight into how we'll feel?

Heir: When we know something, really know it, it only takes a touch of imagination to know how we'll feel.

Sage: Yes, but we don't always know that something, do we?

~ Hatred (Director, Sage)

Director: Tell me, Sage. Do the wise ever hate?

Sage: It's not wise to hate. Hatred clouds the picture.

Director: I've heard people say it makes things clear.

Sage: Well, they're mistaken.

Director: So you would advise Heir not to hate his political enemies?

Sage: Yes, of course.

Director: How should he feel towards them?

Sage: He should pity them.

Director: Pity them? Why?

Sage: Because he's much more able than they are.

Director: But what comes from this pity?

Sage: What do you think comes of it?

Director: Well, no one likes to be an object of pity, or mostly no one. So his enemies will likely resent his pity. Won't that make things harder on him?

Sage: And you think hating them will make things easier?

Director: I don't know. That's why I'm asking.

Sage: Why don't you venture a guess?

Director: Alright. If I had to say, I guess I'd say hatred is a distraction. And it's best to be simply objective.

Sage: So no feelings at all toward your enemies?

Director: None. Look at them coldly and decide what to do.

Sage: And if you decide to hurt them?

Director: Then hit them where it counts. And then you might allow yourself pity — if you'd like to salt the wound.

~ Revenge (Artist, Director, Heir, Sage)

Sage: Revenge is a waste of time. If it happens naturally through the course of events, you can enjoy it. But don't pursue it.

Artist: But what if something as natural as the desire for revenge dictates the course of events?

Sage: We must stand above it.

Director: How do we do that, Sage?

Sage: We focus on the bigger picture.

Heir: What's in that bigger picture?

Sage: Our guiding idea.

Artist: What idea?

Sage: Each of us has our own.

Director: There are billions and billions of ideas?

Sage: No, but each of us puts our own touch on the idea that guides us.

Heir: What idea guides me?

Sage: That's something only you will know.

Artist: What if I'm guided by an idea of revenge?

Sage: Then I feel sorry for you, Artist.

Artist: What if I have two ideas? One of revenge and one of goodwill toward all.

Sage: Then you're in conflict.

Artist: Then let's say my ideas are revenge, and goodwill to all those I don't hate.

Heir: Do you really want revenge?

Artist: Yes. But I don't go out of my way for it. My work is my revenge.

Heir: I like that. I think I'll make my work my revenge, too.

~ The Greedy (Artist, Director, Heir, Sage)

Sage: But who could you possibly want to take revenge on?

Heir: The greedy.

Director: The greedy? Greedy for what?

Heir: Isn't all greed bad?

Director: Oh, I don't know. What about those who are greedy for life?

Heir: I know what you're saying. What's wrong with that? Another example you might raise is being greedy for happiness. And so on. But I do think there's a way greed like that is bad.

Director: How?

Heir: When your unthinking pursuit of what you take as your good harms others.

Sage: Then why don't you just say you want to take revenge on those who harm others?

Heir: Because there's a great amount of harm in the world and I want to have some focus.

Artist: But are you taking revenge for yourself or others?

Heir: I'll make no secret of it. I've felt the ill effects of greed. And I want to avenge all of us so touched.

Director: What kind of greed has touched you, Heir?

Heir: You're not going to believe me.

Director: Try me.

Heir: The greed for love.

Artist: Ha! Who is greedy for your love?

Heir: You might be surprised.

Artist: Oh, I doubt it. But look at your innocent grin! You're teasing — or plotting a light-hearted, harmless revenge.

- Love for Love (Artist, Director, Heir, Sage)

Director: Are the greedy for love in love with love?

Heir: I think that's a very good question. Yes, they often are.

Director: And tell us now — is it much the same thing if we say the greedy for desire desire desire?

Artist: That's a lot of desire.

Heir: Yes, but I think it's true. It's much the same thing.

Director: Which is worse? Being in love with love or having desire for desire?

Heir: I'm not sure which is worse.

Director: What is it about the two that's troublesome?

Heir: Besides the fact that the love or desire is at a remove? It's troublesome when the other assumes that you, too, are in love with love, and so on.

Director: But if it were love at no remove, if it were love without assumption?

Heir: Then it would be much more pure.

Sage: And that's what it takes to win your love? Being pure?

Director: Sage, how can that be enough? For Heir, I think it also takes a certain sort of shyness in a love that's great.

Heir: It's true. If you're shy about a burning love, it shows you have great heart.

Sage: Can you say why?

Heir: Your loving heart must battle the powerful madness of love in your mind. Shyness is a sign the heart has won.

Sage: But is shyness enough to make you love in turn?

Heir: Yes.

Artist: Yes? With an exclusive love?

Heir: Well, no. But with a higher love, a spiritual love — a love worthy of all that restraint.

~ Honor (Artist, Director, Heir, Sage)

Artist: Do you think it can be an honor to be loved?

Heir: Yes, by someone shy and pure.

Artist: But not by any other?

Heir: Well, I wouldn't say that.

Director: Because you can be loved by a friend?

Heir: Yes, that's true.

Director: And a friend can be bold with love?

Heir: Yes, but only so far.

Sage: If it goes too far it's no longer an honor?

Heir: If it goes too far it ceases to be love and becomes unhealthy need.

Sage: And unhealthy need is no honor.

Heir: Not in the least.

Director: How is it with the honors outside of love?

Heir: You mean, for instance, if I'm elected? That sort of honor?

Director: Yes.

Heir: I think it's much the same. A vote from someone needy for me is no honor.

Artist: You'd turn that vote down?

Heir: I would... if I could.

Sage: But then you mustn't appeal to need. You must appeal to love.

Heir: Yes. I want the people to love me as their friend.

Sage: And is that the greatest honor you can imagine?

Heir: Oh, Sage, don't make me choose between their honor and the honor I get from you! What would you have me do? You know I won't undermine my cause.

~ Warmth (Artist, Director, Heir, Sage)

Heir: You can't be a cold fish and get elected.

Director: Why not?

Heir: People neither like nor trust the cold.

Director: But why?

Heir: Because they think the cold will deceive them in the end.

Artist: Ha! Then you just have to pretend to be warm!

Heir: But people see through that.

Artist: So you'll actually be warm? I don't know, Heir.

Heir: What don't you know?

Artist: What are you going to be when you make judgments? Warm or cold?

Heir: Your head must be cold and clear when you decide anything of importance.

Artist: And if you're a leader, won't you often decide things of importance?

Heir: Yes, but you make your decisions on your own.

Artist: And you can be cold when you're on your own?

Heir: Of course.

Artist: But what about when you're with your advisers? Don't you sometimes decide with them? Are they 'people' with whom you must be warm? Or can you be cold?

Heir: It depends.

Artist: On what sort of people they are? Then what about when you're with us, the present company? Can you afford to be cold and clear?

Heir: But why would I want to be cold with my friends?

Artist: Why would you want to make bad decisions with friends?

Sage: He wouldn't, Artist. So he'll just have to find a way to be cold in head and warm in heart at once.

~ Humanity (Artist, Director, Heir, Sage)

Director: If you're warm are you necessarily humane?

Heir: No. Humanity takes more.

Director: What more?

Heir: Compassion, for one.

Sage: But by 'compassion' don't you simply mean warmth?

Heir: Of course not.

Director: Can you have compassion without being warm?

Heir: Yes. Because compassion is concern for the suffering of others. Concern doesn't require warmth. You can be cold and still be concerned.

Director: So tell us. Will you show concern for the suffering of the people?

Heir: Yes, I certainly will. But there's more to the people than suffering. There's also strength. And out of my humanity I'll show concern for that.

Director: You'll make them as strong as they can be?

Heir: Absolutely.

Director: How will you do that?

Heir: By giving them a cause.

Artist: We're stronger when we have a cause?

Heir: Do you have any doubt?

Artist: I have plenty of doubt, my humanitarian friend. And that's fitting — because causes are dubious things!

Director: But maybe Heir has a special cause in mind. Do you, Heir?

Heir: Well, I admit — I haven't worked it all out.

Sage: Oh, don't worry too much about that. Make strength itself the cause. And everything else will fall in line.

~ Naiveté (Artist, Director, Heir, Sage)

Heir: So strength is the cause.

Artist: Yes, yes — but there's a problem with that. Once you get a taste for strength, nothing else tastes as good.

Heir: And what's wrong with that?

Artist: Ha! What's wrong with that? Tell me, Heir. Would you make everyone strong?

Heir: Of course.

Artist: Even the wicked and bad?

Heir: Well, no, of course not.

Artist: But you'd make strong as many of the good as you could?

Heir: Yes.

Artist: And you'd want 'as many of the good as you could' to be the majority?

Heir: No doubt.

Artist: But if they weren't?

Heir: There'd obviously be some trouble, then. But I don't see how this has anything to do with nothing but strength tasting as good.

Artist: Once someone has had a taste, how do you think they'll treat others who try to gain strength, or power, at their expense?

Heir: You think I'm naive. I'm not. I know they'll tend to tyrannize.

Sage: Why will they do that?

Heir: Because they'll do anything to keep the power they've got.

Director: So what's to be done?

Heir: As Artist suggested, you try to give power only to the good.

Sage: Because the good won't tyrannize?

Heir: Oh, of course they will. But would you rather have the tyranny of the bad?

~ Faith (Artist, Director, Heir, Sage)

Heir: I'm sorry, can you say that again?

Sage: You have to keep faith with the electorate.

Heir: Of course.

Sage: And that means your message must be pure.

Heir: No doubt.

Sage: Because if your message isn't pure, there's no faith.

Heir: Yes, but why are you saying all this?

Artist: I suspect he says it because he suspects your faith!

Heir: Buy why?

Sage: There's a danger when you look at things in terms of strength, or power. You might dilute or abandon your faith.

Heir: But why would I do that? Faith can give us power and strength.

Artist: How?

Heir: By providing for our mutual defense.

Director: Can you say more?

Heir: Reciprocal faith, Director. I keep faith with my constituency, and they have faith in me. There's no other way for us all to stay strong.

Director: And do you take pride in this?

Heir: Isn't there always pride in strength?

Director: Not always. Sometimes there's something more, and sometimes there's something less.

Heir: Well, I intend to have proper pride, a pride that's pure and true.

Sage: Then is that your message? Pride?

Heir: Yes. Everyone loves to have some pride. So why not have it through me?

~ Death (Artist, Director, Heir, Sage)

Heir: There are two kinds of death — political death and actual death.

Director: Which is worse?

Heir: Political death. Because to me non-political life is unthinkable.

Artist: Yes, yes. But all life is political, broadly speaking. Even mine!

Heir: How so?

Artist: Well, I live in a political society, my country. I'm subject to the laws. I pay taxes. But here's the most significant thing — I speak the language. I think in the language. I dream in the language. My work is in the language.

Heir: Yes, but it's a stretch to say that language is political.

Artist: Why? What do you think politics is all about?

Heir: Our way of living together.

Artist: Yes! And isn't language the key?

Sage: So what are you saying? There's no such thing as political death?

Artist: No. I'm saying political death happens when you forget your mother tongue.

Sage: Ha, ha! You can't be serious!

Artist: Oh, but I am, Sage — I am! Try forgetting your language and then learning it again from scratch. I'm sure you'll feel it as a sort of death followed by rebirth. And no, this doesn't happen overnight. It takes years and years to forget and then relearn.

Director: And when you've learned?

Artist: You stand apart.

Heir: Outside politics?

Artist: Outside the old politics.

Director: And what do you do in this new found place?

Artist: You encourage others to come. And you wait.

~ Precision (Artist, Director, Heir, Sage)

Artist: Overly precise language is deadly.

Heir: How so?

Artist: It's suffocating.

Director: But what about language that's not precise enough?

Artist: It's sloppy, and not very helpful.

Sage: So we're looking for just the right amount of precision.

Heir: How will we know what that is?

Artist: We'll know because we get our message across. No more and no less.

Director: But what if our message itself is ambiguous? Do we need ambiguous language?

Artist: An ambiguous message isn't really a message. It might be more of a hint.

Heir: But can't you give hints in perfectly clear language?

Sage: Heir has a point. Can't you?

Artist: Of course you can.

Heir: Then why not always be perfectly clear but not too precise?

Director: I think we should.

Heir: Give us an example.

Director: Okay. I want you to run. Clear enough?

Heir: Of course. You want me to run for office.

Artist: But it could also mean he wants you to run from office, to run away. So context is everything here.

Sage: But context, too, can be deadly. No?

Artist: Of course it can — when it tries to force meanings on us that run counter to sense.

~ Prophecy (Artist, Sage)

Artist: Sage, do you ever dabble in prophecy?

Sage: What? Of course not.

Artist: But isn't that what the wise do?

Sage: Artist, I don't know where you're getting your information. But the answer is a definite no.

Artist: Well, I like to dabble in prophecy now and then. I do it in my works.

Sage: And do your prophecies ever turn out correct?

Artist: For the most part.

Sage: For the most part? That's an amazing thing. How do you do it?

Artist: I leave things nice and vague. That way most everyone is satisfied.

Sage: What about those who are skeptical about prophecy?

Artist: They're satisfied I'm no prophet. You see? Everyone is happy. But I don't see why the wise don't prophesy.

Sage: The wise know better.

Artist: What do they know?

Sage: To keep what they know of the future to themselves, sharing only with the rare individual.

Artist: But what do they know of the future?

Sage: What anyone with a good dose of sense can puzzle out.

Artist: That must be quite some dose you're talking about. But with whom would the wise share? People who need to know?

Sage: Yes, but needing to know may be different than what you think.

Artist: What do you think I think?

Sage: That you're someone who needs to know.

~ Timeless (Director, Sage)

Director: Sage, have you ever heard wisdom is timeless?

Sage: Yes, I have.

Director: Is it true?

Sage: For some things, yes.

Director: What things?

Sage: Things concerning human nature.

Director: Because human nature never changes?

Sage: That's right.

Director: And that's across the millennia, going far back into the earliest human history, say at least a few hundred thousand years?

Sage: Well, I'm not sure about that.

Director: But if you're not sure about that how can you be sure wisdom is timeless?

Sage: Because we're speaking relatively.

Director: Relative to the last few thousand years or so?

Sage: Yes.

Director: But didn't people believe different things and live in different cultures just a few thousand years ago?

Sage: True.

Director: So isn't it possible that what was wise for them might not be wise for us?

Sage: What do you want me to say, Director?

Director: That wisdom, as we know it, is limited to a relatively small range of time.

Sage: In the particulars, perhaps. But wisdom as wisdom has always been around. And always will be around — as long as humans exist. But what about philosophy?

Director: Philosophy's existence has no guarantee. So every minute counts.

~ Expertise (Artist, Director, Heir, Sage)

Director: Is wisdom expertise?

Heir: No, I wouldn't say it is.

Sage: Why not?

Heir: Because expertise means you're knowledgeable in a particular topic.

Director: What if you're knowledgeable in many topics?

Heir: Then you have a wide range of expertise.

Director: Can that wide range of expertise add up to wisdom?

Heir: I don't know, Director. I really don't think of expertise when I think about wisdom.

Director: What do you think about?

Heir: A certain way of knowing.

Artist: But didn't you just say experts are knowledgeable?

Heir: Yes, but I'm distinguishing between knowing and being knowledgeable, if that makes sense.

Director: What do the wise know?

Heir: I'm having a hard time putting my finger on it.

Director: Is it a knowing about people or things?

Heir: People.

Director: And what can we know about people?

Artist: I'll tell you. How to handle them. How to deal with them.

Sage: And this handling and dealing doesn't admit of expertise?

Heir: When it comes to the wise? No, I don't think it does.

Sage: Why, Heir?

Heir: Because if it did, it would seem too... cold.

~ Intoxicated (Director, Heir, Sage)

Sage: Sober heads prevail.

Heir: Isn't the saying, cooler heads prevail?

Sage: What difference does it make?

Heir: Well, you can be intoxicated and still keep cool. I do it all the time.

Sage: That's because the times you've been intoxicated, you haven't had to deal with serious conflict.

Heir: Not so! I've dealt with plenty of conflict — and dealt with it well.

Director: Better than when you're sober?

Heir: Well, it's hard to say, Director. We'd have to compare like to like — and there's nothing quite like the sorts of scrapes I get into when I'm drunk!

Director: Why?

Heir: Because the others around me are drunk. And they're the source of the trouble.

Sage: But how do you know you're not the source? Maybe you say inflammatory things and those around you react.

Heir: No, I'd know if that were the case. It's not.

Director: Tell me, Heir. Do you listen well when you're drinking?

Heir: Stick around and see for yourself! But you didn't ask me whether I like to listen to those who are sober or those who are drunk.

Director: Which do you prefer?

Heir: It depends on the person and what they have to say. Some people say different things when sober and when drunk, you know. But others say the same thing either way. And I'll tell you — I only fully accept the counsel of the latter!

Sage: You didn't quite answer the question. But one thing is clear. You're putting us to the test with the truth serum you're serving here tonight!

Heir: Ha, ha! I am! I'm putting all my guests to the test. I want to know what they really think, and whether they need to be coaxed — to share it with me.

~ Probing (Artist, Director, Sage)

Artist: People are more open when they've had a couple of drinks.

Director: Then that's a good time to probe.

Sage: What kind of probing are you talking about, Director?

Director: Oh, for anything you might want to know.

Sage: Give us an example.

Director: What someone truly thinks about a particular political opinion.

Artist: You're more likely to get the full truth about that when they're loose.

Director: Yes.

Sage: But what else would you probe for?

Director: For how firmly attached they are to their opinion.

Sage: Because you want to know if you can win them over to your side?

Director: Win them over to the cause. Yes.

Sage: And what else would you try to know?

Director: What else is there?

Sage: What? You're going to claim that political opinions are the only things worth knowing?

Director: Do you think we should probe into their private life? Their love life, say?

Artist: Ha! Sure! Why not? And I wouldn't be surprised if we find that a great many political opinions derive from a person's love life, or lack thereof — and I don't just mean love in the romantic sense.

Director: So love is fair game?

Sage: It's fair enough. But is there anything else to probe for while we're at it?

Artist: Honestly? I wouldn't mind hearing a little truth about what people think... about my work. But you ask them that. It doesn't do for me to show too much interest here!

~ Roots (Artist, Director, Heir, Sage)

Heir: Here are the drinks! Oh, Artist! I didn't get one for you.

Artist: No worries. I'm sure a server will be by any minute.

Director: We were just discussing how we probe others, Heir.

Heir: Ah, that's something I do all the time.

Sage: What do you probe for?

Heir: A person's roots.

Artist: Roots? What does that mean?

Heir: Literally, they're what nourishes them.

Director: So you talk about food?

Heir: Ha, ha. Yes, in a way. Food for the soul. Food for thought.

Director: What's the difference between the two?

Heir: Oh, there's really no difference.

Artist: What's an example of this kind of food?

Heir: Your art!

Artist: Bah, don't flatter me.

Sage: You don't think art is a kind of nourishing food?

Artist: Of course I do. But some art is a light snack and some art is a heavy meal. So, Heir, tell me what kind mine is — if you don't mind my being so bold.

Heir: Not at all. Yours is an exquisite many-course meal. One that leaves you feeling satisfied yet light.

Director: Has he hit it right on the head, or struck the perfect flattering tone?

Artist: Who can say? But what other food is there? We can't live on art alone.

Heir: That's what Director is for. Philosophy is food. And not to leave you out, Sage — wisdom, too, is food. Wisdom, philosophy, art. The rest is just the needs... of the body.

~ Flexibility (Artist, Director, Heir, Sage)

Sage: But aren't we forgetting something? Love. Love nourishes you.

Heir: Ah, how could we have forgotten? Thank you, Sage.

Director: But I wonder if love is somehow different.

Heir: How so?

Director: The other three — art, philosophy, and wisdom — require a degree of flexibility. No?

Sage: What do you mean?

Director: Artist, don't you want your work to increase the mental flexibility of your audience?

Artist: Yes, of course.

Director: And you do that by putting in things that call for a stretch?

Artist: Without a stretch my work is of no interest.

Director: And I can say it's the same for philosophy. No stretch, no interest. But what about wisdom?

Sage: It's always wise to be flexible — except for when you need to stand firm.

Director: Alright. Now let's turn to love. Does it require flexibility?

Heir: Yes, of course it does. But this only states the obvious. We all need to be flexible when dealing with other human beings, especially those we love.

Director: But, Heir, why must we be especially flexible with those we love?

Sage: I can answer that. It's because love demands more of us than anything.

Director: And if we're rigid when we face those demands, we'll break?

Sage: I think that puts it well.

Artist: Yes, Sage. But when would you be not rigid, but firm, with the one you love?

Sage: When they're being inflexible with me.

~ Experimentation (Artist, Director, Heir, Sage)

Heir: I think the most important reason to be flexible is so you can experiment freely.

Sage: Yes, but we can't be too free.

Artist: Why not? Because we'll learn something we don't want to know?

Director: What's something we don't want to know, Artist?

Artist: Something that calls our beliefs into question.

Director: But are you suggesting we do want to call our beliefs into question?

Artist: Yes! What's the point of experimenting freely if not to learn new things?

Director: And new things always challenge our beliefs?

Artist: In some way, shape, or form? Yes. Don't you agree, Heir?

Heir: Not necessarily. You can learn something new that bolsters your belief.

Sage: Yes, that's a very good point. But you should still be careful with your experiments.

Artist: Why?

Sage: From some experiments you can never recover.

Director: You mean like experimenting with highly addictive drugs?

Sage: Yes. Your experiment proves to be a trap.

Heir: But not everyone is trapped.

Sage: True. But so many are.

Director: Hmm. Heir, what kind of free experimentation did you have in mind?

Heir: The experiment of being open to new people, people unlike you.

Director: You mean, you give them a chance? Well, that should suit you well in your campaign.

Artist: Yes, Heir, it should. But if you come to feel trapped, you can count on us to experiment freely, quite freely in fact — on ways to break you free.

~ Selflessness (Director, Sage)

Sage: Taken to the extreme, Heir's experimentation with people leads to nothing other than selflessness.

Director: Selflessness? But do you think that's good or bad?

Sage: Bad! We can be too open to others. And when we are we lose ourselves.

Director: So Heir needs to find a way to be open but keep his self?

Sage: Yes, and he does that by having backbone.

Director: How will he know if he's losing his backbone?

Sage: It's simple. He won't be standing straight and tall.

Director: You mean, for instance, if he bends down to listen to others?

Sage: Yes. And if he does, he must straighten right back up again.

Director: Then what's the hope?

Sage: The hope? Why, that the other will learn to stand up tall, as well.

Director: And if he or she doesn't?

Sage: It's time to move on.

Director: But you don't think Heir needs to give them more of a chance?

Sage: I think one chance is enough. But, in a way, they have more than a chance. Heir serves as an example to them.

Director: An example they can follow even though he's gone?

Sage: Precisely.

Director: Should Heir return to see if they ever stood up?

Sage: He can. And if they have, he can keep on coming back.

Director: But if they haven't?

Sage: He needs to learn to leave them — well enough alone.

~ Responsibility (Director, Heir, Sage)

Director: Heir, are you responsible to those you understand?

Heir: I think you are, to some degree.

Director: Why?

Heir: Because whoever you understand is, in a sense, a part of you. And you're always responsible to yourself.

Director: Even if you don't understand yourself?

Heir: You're responsible to come to understand yourself.

Director: In whole or in part?

Heir: Well, you start with the parts and work your way up to the whole.

Director: Hmm. Just to be clear. Are we saying those we've understood can be part of our whole?

Heir: We are.

Director: But what if we never make them part of us? Can we be whole?

Sage: No, Director, no one can be whole without others.

Heir: Not even if you really understand and are responsible to yourself?

Sage: And you're irresponsible toward all others?

Heir: Aren't you irresponsible only if you understand but turn away? If you don't understand, you're neither responsible nor irresponsible. You just don't know.

Sage: We have a responsibility to know. I'm sure Director agrees.

Director: Know what?

Sage: The other!

Director: But what about the other must we know? Everything?

Sage: No, of course not everything.

Heir: Then how can we understand?

~ Causes (Artist, Director, Heir, Sage)

Artist: There are two types of cause. Cause as in cause and effect, which we can call scientific cause. And cause as in a political movement.

Heir: Yes, but political movements hope to cause a certain effect. And science as a whole has a cause, and it's political in nature.

Director: Do you think the cause of science as a whole, its political cause, can affect its findings concerning cause and effect?

Heir: You mean, does the political base of science affect its results? How could it not?

Artist: Yes, yes — but problems like that aside, I prefer science and its cause.

Heir: Why?

Artist: The politics of science is less political, if that makes sense.

Sage: Of course that doesn't make sense. Politics is politics.

Heir: And politics limits what scientists can do. They're not as free as some would like to think.

Director: So you two don't prefer science?

Sage: To the contrary, Director. I prefer science.

Director: Why?

Sage: Because science likes to think of itself as outside of politics.

Director: But you don't think it's outside?

Sage: No, I don't.

Artist: Ha! Then you'd better explain.

Sage: When a cause conceives of itself as being outside, even though it's not, it creates possibilities. It opens things up.

Director: So what should we do if we discover a new cause, a cause that thinks it stands outside?

Sage: We should nourish it. Because that's when things get interesting again.

~ Equality (Artist, Director, Heir, Sage)

Artist: Yes, sure — we're all equal. But who would say people are equal in every sense?

Heir: They're equal in one sense and unequal in another.

Director: What's the one sense?

Heir: We're all citizens, we're all human beings.

Director: And the other sense?

Artist: Ha! The other sense is what really counts. It's the difference between wisdom and folly!

Director: Heir? Is that what really counts?

Heir: Both senses count. But Artist has a point.

Director: Sage?

Sage: I agree.

Director: So, just to be clear — what does this mean? That we're equal for political purposes? The rights of the citizen and the rights of all? But when it comes to what we are, beyond or behind all that, we're unequal?

Heir: Yes.

Director: Should we be unequal?

Heir: You're asking if not everyone should be wise?

Director: Yes. Sage, what do you think?

Sage: I believe the more who are wise, the better off we'll all be.

Artist: You say that as if there's simply wisdom or not. Don't you recognize degrees?

Heir: We have to recognize degrees. After all, aren't some of the wise always wiser than others?

Sage: If so, it's really too bad. Because then the wise miss out on something wonderful. Complete equality among their peers.

~ Rarity (Artist, Director, Heir, Sage)

Artist: Wisdom is necessarily rare.

Director: You mean everyone can't be wise?

Artist: Yes, it's like it is at the races. Not all the horses can win.

Sage: But wisdom isn't about competing.

Heir: What's it about?

Sage: Choosing wisely and living well.

Artist: And everyone can choose wisely and live well?

Sage: That's my belief. Why? Do you believe the world is a zero sum game? If I do well, someone else must do poorly?

Artist: No, I don't believe that. Not absolutely. But I think you're naive about this, Sage.

Sage: How so?

Artist: Being wise gives you an advantage over others. If everyone is wise, that advantage disappears. And then what's the point of wisdom?

Sage: Artist, it's as I said. Wisdom is for the sake of living well.

Heir: I think Sage is right.

Artist: Yes, yes. But that only confirms that the wise have always been few. Not many live well, you know.

Heir: Oh, I don't know. More might live well than we think.

Artist: Ha! And why do you think that?

Heir: Because who's to judge who truly lives well?

Director: But don't we all have to judge this to the best of our knowledge?

Heir: Why would you say that?

Sage: I know why. Because we all hope to live well, and long for examples of what this means.

~ Sayings (Artist, Director, Sage)

Director: Do the wise let others into their wisdom?

Sage: I'm not sure what you mean by 'into their wisdom', Director. But the wise share.

Artist: Ha! I know what they share. Sayings.

Director: Sayings?

Artist: Yes, yes. 'A penny saved is a penny earned.' That sort of thing.

Sage: I don't have any sayings like that.

Artist: Not yet, maybe, but you probably will.

Director: And what's the good of sayings?

Artist: People think this is how the wise really think. So they take the sayings to heart and try to learn from them.

Director: But shouldn't they try to learn from them? And if they learn, won't they be wise?

Artist: In a sense. But as I suggested — not in the way of the wise.

Sage: How do you think the wise really think?

Artist: I think they think of themselves and only themselves. And I have no problem with that. But then they pretend to think of others when they offer up their sayings.

Director: How do sayings make them seem to think of others?

Artist: By making them seem to offer up all of their wisdom, their core.

Sage: And you're sure they don't offer this up?

Artist: Ha, of course!

Sage: Why wouldn't they?

Artist: Because you have to offer up something people can believe.

Sage: And people can't believe true wisdom from the core?

Artist: Those who can are few. And they already know true wisdom at first hand.

~ Misunderstanding (Artist, Director, Sage)

Artist: Sometimes it's best to misunderstand.

Sage: What do you mean?

Artist: I mean, sometimes things work out better when you pretend to misunderstand.

Sage: Why in the world would you say that?

Artist: Because it's true, Sage. Can't you imagine a situation that calls for misunderstanding?

Sage: Honestly? No.

Artist: Director?

Director: Let me see if I understand. You're saying that understanding, or I should say open understanding, can be bad?

Artist: Yes.

Director: Hmm. Well, let's look at an example. Suppose you stole cookies from the cookie jar. And the one who owns the cookies comes in with the jar and says, 'Can you believe it? Who would do that?' And you understand full well, but you pretend not to and say, 'I know, who would have left the lights on all night?' Is that what you mean?

Artist: Yes, yes — but I don't like your example. You're suggesting misunderstanding is for when we've done something wrong.

Director: Well, then when else should we misunderstand?

Artist: When we're being ironic.

Director: Ah. So what's an example?

Sage: I can think of one now. An advisee might be frustrated with me. And this person is passive aggressive and drops all sorts of hints that I'm no good. I misunderstand those hints as having nothing to do with me, and carry on.

Director: Is that good practice?

Sage: If it allows us to stay focused on the greater goal? I'd say yes. Because when we deal with the major issue, the minor one often withers away.

- Distance (Artist, Director, Sage)

Artist: Another benefit of irony is that it creates distance.

Sage: Yes, but that's a problem.

Director: How so?

Sage: Closeness to the advisee helps the process.

Director: How?

Sage: You really understand what they're going through when you're close.

Director: And they really understand what you're going through?

Sage: Well, not exactly.

Director: Then there's some distance inherent to the process. I mean, there would be no distance if you knew what they were going through and they knew what you were going through in all the aspects of your life.

Sage: True. Then we'd be friends.

Artist: Ha! You'd have no distance between friends?

Sage: What good is distance?

Artist: It allows you room to breathe!

Director: Sage, if you don't mind my asking — how many zero-distance friends do you have?

Sage: I have... none.

Director: But you do have friends?

Sage: Of course! I just wish they were zero distance, as you say.

Director: Why aren't they?

Artist: I know why. Because he scares them off! But I also know what he really wants.

Sage: And what's that?

Artist: Passionate love between friends.

~ Mistakes (Artist, Director, Sage)

Artist: As with misunderstanding, so too is it with mistakes.

Sage: You're suggesting there are times when we should make intentional mistakes?

Artist: Yes. I do it all the time in my works.

Sage: But that just sounds like an insurance plan.

Artist: How so?

Sage: If the reader knows your characters might intentionally make mistakes, every time you the author make a mistake, the reader will think the character did it on purpose.

Artist: No, no — that's not how it works. The reader has to see why the character makes a mistake, not just that the character makes one.

Sage: So why would a character of yours make a mistake?

Artist: To call attention to a problem.

Sage: How does making a mistake do that?

Artist: If you know the character knows better, then you know the character is making an intentional mistake. And you know this is problematic. So you the reader must ask: What about this situation calls for a mistake?

Sage: And what calls for a mistake?

Artist: Oh, it could be anything. This technique is just a tool. How you use it and what it means depend on your plot.

Director: Tell us, Artist. How does an intentional mistake differ from a lie?

Artist: Essentially? I suppose it doesn't.

Director: Now, when a lie is found out it makes you look bad. But what about a mistake?

Artist: Mistakes are forgiven more readily than lies. But not if it's clear you made them on purpose. So the question is: Who would ever accuse you of that?

Sage: Artist, that's easy. Someone who knows you all too well.

Director: Or maybe not well enough.

~ Professionals and Amateurs (Artist, Director, Heir, Sage)

Director: Sage, do you consider yourself a professional adviser?

Sage: Well, it is my full time work.

Artist: Yes, but you don't take any money for it.

Heir: Do you have to take money to be a professional?

Artist: Don't you?

Director: Should we say Sage is an amateur?

Heir: No, he has too much wisdom to be an amateur, as far as I'm concerned.

Director: Then maybe he's some sort of hybrid with the best of both worlds?

Sage: Director, you flatter me. It's also possible that I'm the worst of both worlds.

Director: What's the bad part of being a professional?

Sage: You come to believe you're the expert, that you know it all.

Director: And what's the bad part of being an amateur?

Sage: You lack the rigor a profession demands.

Director: Heir, you've been advised by Sage. Does he think he knows it all?

Heir: Absolutely not.

Director: And does he lack rigor?

Heir: Not at all.

Director: So, Sage, it seems you're not the worst of both worlds.

Sage: Yes, but what about you, Director? Are you a professional or amateur philosopher?

Director: I think I'm neither, just like you. I take no money but practice all the time. And I like to think I don't represent the worst of both those worlds.

Heir: Of course you don't. But now we see you two have much in common! So do the decent thing — and help each other out.

~ Rivals (Artist, Director, Heir, Sage)

Artist: Help each other out? Ha! They're rivals!

Heir: Why do you say that?

Artist: If their ways are so alike can they really be anything but?

Heir: But philosophy is the love of wisdom!

Artist: Yes, but did you bother to ask if wisdom is the love of philosophy?

Sage: Wisdom loves itself. If philosophy brings wisdom, then wisdom will love it, too.

Heir: Can philosophy bring wisdom?

Director: It can certainly try. But let's choose a topic and see.

Sage: Fine. Let's talk about the wisdom in loving your friends.

Director: Hmm. I'm not sure what kind of wisdom I have here.

Sage: How so?

Director: Tell me this. How do I know what friends to love?

Sage: You're going to question me? I thought you were trying to bring wisdom.

Director: But that's my way of bringing wisdom.

Artist: Ha! It seems we have a problem already. But I'll answer you, Director. You know what friends to love because you should love them all.

Director: Yes. But some friends are better than others. Do I love them more?

Artist: That's only natural. And you should love your best friend most.

Director: Now here's the test. Is it wise to let your friends know where they stand?

Sage: In how much you love them? No, certainly not!

Director: Well, that's where we part company, Sage.

Sage: You'd make things clear and risk hurting the feelings of those you love less?

Director: The ones I love less aren't so easily hurt, which makes me... love them more.

- Therapy (Artist, Director, Heir, Sage)

Director: How would you define therapy, Sage?

Sage: As healing talk.

Heir: And he would know. He does more than give good advice. His talk heals.

Artist: But are you healed, or do you have more healing to do?

Heir: It's funny you should ask. Sage and I were just talking about that the other day. I'm healed.

Artist: So you don't want to see him anymore?

Heir: Of course I do. As a friend.

Director: That must require some adjustment.

Sage: Why do you say that, Director?

Director: Because wasn't the focus always on Heir?

Sage: True.

Director: On his well-being?

Sage: Yes. And now you're wondering if we'll focus, at least in part, on my well-being?

Director: Will you?

Sage: I suppose we should.

Artist: But you have a hard habit to break — talking about others and not yourself.

Sage: Then I'll learn to break it.

Artist: You'll have to sacrifice your position of power, you know.

Sage: Power? You think not speaking about yourself amounts to power?

Artist: Of course! Just ask Heir.

Heir: Yes, but now that we're through we'll share the power.

Artist: Ah, but that's always easier said than done.

- Money (Artist, Director, Heir, Sage)

Artist: I don't understand why you don't take money.

Sage: I don't want it to cloud things up.

Artist: You don't want your advisees to think that's why you're talking to them?

Sage: Precisely.

Director: But why are you talking to them?

Sage: Because I want to help, Director.

Heir: I don't believe you don't get paid for your help, Sage.

Sage: What do you mean?

Heir: Your pay is other than money.

Sage: Well, I'm satisfied whenever I can be of use.

Heir: Then that's your pay. And it's worth more than money, right?

Sage: Yes.

Artist: Do you look down on those who do take money?

Sage: Of course not. Most of them have no choice. And many of them volunteer time beyond their normal work.

Artist: I would never give art for free, even if I had enough money that it didn't matter.

Sage: Why not?

Artist: Because I value my work. And others who value it in turn can respect why I want money. It's more honest that way.

Sage: Honest? You don't think my work is honest?

Artist: I'll tell you what I think, in no uncertain terms. There's something dishonest in what you do.

Sage: You must be kidding! What on earth would make me less than honest?

Artist: A lack of competence coupled with arrogance — which generally amounts to rot.

~ Satisfaction (Artist, Director, Heir, Sage)

Sage: So you think I'm rotten?

Heir: No one thinks you're rotten, Sage. Least of all Artist.

Artist: Why do you think that is?

Heir: Because you know full well Sage is competent and not the least bit arrogant.

Director: Hmm. Artist, can you say more about why you insist on always taking money for your work?

Artist: I insist, in part, because it obscures my deeper satisfaction.

Sage: Why would you want it to do that?

Artist: Because the amount of satisfaction I derive from my work is obscene.

Heir: How can satisfaction be obscene?

Artist: I hope you find out one day.

Sage: So you want people to think you're doing it for the money?

Artist: I want certain people to think I'm doing it for the money.

Heir: But that's just crazy. Why is everyone talking so crazy today?

Director: Because they haven't come over to philosophy.

Artist: Ha!

Director: You may laugh, my friend. But do you think philosophers have to obscure their deepest satisfaction?

Heir: Philosophers are unashamed?

Director: Yes. And, in fact, they think there's something sly in being ashamed.

Artist: Now I'm sly? But who says I'm ashamed? I obscure my satisfaction for other reasons, reasons that have nothing to do with shame.

Heir: What reasons, Artist?

Artist: Reasons having to do with prudence... and a peculiar sort of pride.

- Resistance (Artist, Director, Sage)

Director: So, Artist and Sage, are you ready to come over to philosophy?

Sage: What would that mean, exactly?

Director: Exactly? I'm afraid I don't have an 'exactly' sort of answer for you.

Sage: You want us to come over sight unseen?

Director: You haven't seen philosophy in me?

Sage: Yes, I suppose I have. But, Director, I suspect it goes nowhere.

Director: Nowhere? How so?

Sage: When is the last time you created a theory that explains things, one that sticks, and changes the way people think?

Director: Well, never. But I have helped change the way people think.

Artist: Tell us, Director. Did they resist?

Director: No.

Sage: How can that be? Anytime I try to change the way someone thinks I run into terrible resistance.

Director: Maybe you're talking to the wrong people.

Sage: And to whom should I speak?

Director: Those who truly want to change and are almost there.

Sage: Then why do they need me?

Director: Sometimes people just need a little encouragement.

Sage: And that's all you do? Offer some encouragement?

Director: That's it.

Sage: And you take great satisfaction in that?

Director: I do. And I'm often more satisfied than those who try to do something more. Because there's beauty in letting people change however they will.

~ Acceptance (Artist, Director, Heir, Sage)

Sage: We should accept people for who they are.

Artist: Even if we don't like them?

Sage: We accept that we don't like them.

Artist: Ha! And how does that really differ from not accepting them?

Sage: In not accepting them we deny them their right to be who they are.

Artist: And should we grant them that right even if they don't grant it to us?

Sage: Two wrongs don't make a right.

Artist: But what if granting them their right hurts us in our fight?

Heir: Our fight?

Artist: Our fight against what they are! Or don't you think we have to fight that fight, the fight against those who don't grant us our right?

Heir: Of course we have to fight that fight. But can't we both accept them and fight them at once?

Director: Tell us, Heir. How can we accept something we fight? Wouldn't acceptance mean, precisely, we don't fight?

Heir: If we can accept that they oppose us, we can accept that we must fight.

Director: Artist, what do you think about that?

Artist: It's sophistry. We either accept or fight — but never both at once. To say otherwise is just a lie.

Sage: I'm wondering something, Artist. You said who our enemy is. But who are we that we're not accepted, that we're not given our right?

Artist: You make it sound like it's our fault! But I'll tell you, Sage. We're those who accept everyone — except those who won't accept us.

Heir: We accept everyone? Even the bad?

Artist: You must be teasing, because I know you know — the bad never accept the good.

- Impressions (Artist, Director, Sage)

Artist: Heir needs to make a good, powerful impression. So when he talks about his true friends he has to make it clear he's talking about more than a handful. He has to talk about a great many friends who will help him carry the day.

Sage: I disagree. I think he needs to give the impression that each person he's talking to is part of his special small handful of friends.

Artist: Ah, that's the oldest political lie there is!

Sage: That's because it works.

Director: But why lie? Why not say he wants people to organize into many little bands of friends who support the cause? Then there's greatness and intimacy both.

Artist: Why would they agree to do that?

Director: Because they want a better world.

Artist: Ha! Now you've lost your mind.

Director: You don't want a better world?

Artist: Of course I do. Why, do I not give that impression?

Sage: You often give a cynical impression.

Artist: Better that than the impression of a fool.

Director: You really don't think people can organize themselves toward a greater goal?

Artist: It's not that I think they can't. It's that I'm not sure where it all ends.

Sage: It ends in a better place.

Artist: But what if it doesn't? What if it ends in a much worse place — and everyone is organized toward that end?

Sage: Why would people organize for a worse world? It makes no sense.

Artist: I'm saying it might be a better world for them — but not for us!

Sage: If that's what you believe, you're on the wrong side. But can you honestly say that's the impression you get from Heir? That that's how he'd have it all end?

~ Pity (Artist, Director, Sage)

Artist: Pity can kill you.

Sage: Why would you say that?

Artist: Tell me. Do you feel awful when you pity?

Sage: I do. I feel awful for the other.

Artist: But do you also feel pleased?

Sage: How so?

Artist: You feel you're better off than the one you pity.

Sage: If I'm honest? I suppose that's sometimes true, to some small extent.

Artist: Well, it's that mixture of feeling awful and feeling pleased that can kill.

Director: Because the pleasure keeps you coming back for more?

Artist: Yes. And the awfulness takes its toll.

Director: But what if it didn't? What if you were only pleased? Is that possible?

Artist: It's certainly possible. In fact, that's how I feel all the time.

Sage: But, Artist, you can't mean that.

Artist: Of course I can.

Sage: Do you actually go around searching for people to pity?

Artist: Yes, and I feel better when I find them.

Sage: Oh, you're not serious. But tell us how you avoid feeling awful.

Artist: I'll let you in on the secret. I never imagine myself in their place.

Sage: Now I know you're teasing us.

Artist: And how do you know that?

Sage: You live by your imagination!

Artist: Yes, but who says I can't rein it in?

~ Power (Director, Sage)

Sage: Pity can involve power, you know.

Director: Power for whom? The one who pities or the one who is pitied?

Sage: The one who is pitied.

Director: Really? And how does that work?

Sage: The one who is pitied can manipulate the other.

Director: Is that what power is all about? Manipulation?

Sage: I wouldn't say it's what it's all about. But it's certainly an exercise of power.

Director: And the manipulated one needs power in order to break free?

Sage: That one must be powerful enough to stop pitying when it's clear what's going on.

Director: It's not an easy thing to stop pitying?

Sage: It's not. Some go on pitying even though they know they're being manipulated.

Director: Because they're weak?

Sage: Yes. But the funny thing is they think they're strong.

Director: Strong? How so?

Sage: They think it takes strength to go on pitying in the face of evident manipulation.

Director: But why would anyone want to use up their strength that way?

Sage: They hope to turn the tables and gain a degree of power over the one they pity.

Director: To what end?

Sage: To be able to help. Or to show that two can play the game.

Director: The game? But that's crazy, Sage. Are you sure you've got it right?

Sage: I am. And I'm not ashamed to admit I know a bit about these things first hand.

Director: Then you do well to warn others about them, so they can learn from where you went wrong.

- Boredom (Artist, Director, Heir, Sage)

Heir: I pity those who bore easily.

Sage: Why?

Heir: Because we all have the power never to be bored.

Artist: Never? What's the secret?

Heir: To think of the most difficult thing you can, something you'd like to do, and then try to do it.

Director: And I take it running for office is your most difficult thing.

Heir: Yes. Now I'd like to know what the most difficult thing is for the three of you.

Sage: Advising another is the most difficult thing I can do.

Artist: Creating my next work is the most difficult thing I can do.

Heir: Director?

Director: The most difficult thing I can do is to come to agreement with others.

Artist: Ha! But you're not telling the whole story. There's agreement and then there's apparent agreement.

Director: Why would I want to apparently agree?

Artist: I think you do it because it's exhausting to disagree all the time.

Sage: Apparent agreement must get boring, Director.

Director: So what are you suggesting? That open disagreement is actually what I love, what keeps me from being bored?

Heir: Knowing you, you wouldn't disagree for the sake of disagreement. So why do you disagree?

Director: Because I want to get at the truth. That's what keeps me from being bored.

Sage: Well, I think that's what Artist and I at bottom do, too — get at the truth.

Director: But what about Heir? Is that his end goal, too? Can it be his end goal, too?

~ Lies (Artist, Heir)

Artist: Honesty may be the best policy. But when is it wise to lie?

Heir: It's never wise to lie.

Artist: Ha! You just did. And look at you smirk!

Heir: You tell me when it's wise to lie, Artist.

Artist: When the benefits of the lie outweigh its cost.

Heir: Name one benefit of a lie.

Artist: Oh, Heir, it all depends on the individual case. But I can tell you the cost.

Heir: Let me guess. The truth.

Artist: Yes. And how heavy a cost do you think that is? Sometimes heavier than others?

Heir: Yes, I think that's true.

Artist: So if there's a significant benefit, and the cost is low, isn't it wise to lie?

Heir: But being found out is a real problem.

Artist: And so you wouldn't, for instance, lie to the voters?

Heir: I wouldn't.

Artist: But you would lie to me?

Heir: You know I'd care if you found out.

Artist: But what if the risk were low and the lie were really in your interest?

Heir: Can a lie ever really be in your interest?

Artist: Of course! You know this, you and your 'moderate' lies.

Heir: Give me an example.

Artist: You lie to your captors in order to set yourself free.

Heir: But what if the lie backfires and only makes things worse?

Artist: That's possible, of course. But it's a poor excuse not to try.

~ Perplexity (Director, Sage)

Director: Wisdom perplexes me, Sage.

Sage: But, Director, it's the simplest thing in the world!

Director: How can that be? If it were so simple why would anyone not be wise?

Sage: Because it's not easy to be simple.

Director: And that's why I'm perplexed? Because wisdom is hard?

Sage: Yes. But there's more to it than that.

Director: How so?

Sage: When we don't want to do something hard we make excuses.

Director: And excuses complicate things?

Sage: Definitely.

Director: So if I stop making excuses I might not become wise but at least I'll stop being perplexed?

Sage: Yes.

Director: Are you ever perplexed?

Sage: Never.

Director: You always know what to think, what to do?

Sage: Well, it's not always immediately obvious. But yes.

Director: That's what I admire most about wisdom. But once you've thought, once you've done — do you ever doubt?

Sage: Doubt after the fact does no good. In fact, such doubt often renders you perplexed.

Director: So no excuses before, and afterwards no doubt?

Sage: Yes, Director. And with this you'll find yourself relieved — and on your way to being wise.

~ Adventure (Director, Heir, Sage)

Director: What makes you want to run?

Heir: Oh, many things. But the main reason? Adventure.

Director: I suspected as much. Sage, is that a good reason to run?

Sage: As good a reason as any.

Director: Really? I thought you'd say adventure isn't wise.

Sage: If adventure makes you happy, it's wise to be adventurous.

Director: Because wisdom is all about happiness?

Sage: Wisdom is all about life. And happiness is a major part of life.

Director: Are you adventurous?

Sage: I have my little adventures. How about you?

Director: Many of the conversations I have are adventures.

Sage: What makes them so?

Director: What's at stake.

Sage: And what's at stake?

Director: The truth. And what's more exciting than that?

Heir: Running for office. What's more exciting for you, Sage?

Sage: Helping people.

Director: Too bad we can't combine all three.

Sage: Yes. But, you know, helping people involves the truth.

Director: But what about running for office?

Heir: Ha, ha. You know there can be truth and help in that.

Director: I can see how there might be some truth. But help?

Heir: You can give the people a voice! And don't tell me you don't think that helps.

~ Bonds (Director, Sage)

Director: Tell me, Sage. Do the wise form bonds?

Sage: Bonds with others? Of course.

Director: What sort of others?

Sage: Friends, family.

Director: How do the wise decide, in individual cases, who they'll form bonds with?

Sage: It just happens.

Director: Really? The wise have no control over their bonds?

Sage: Well, they can always break a bond.

Director: Why would they want to do that?

Sage: Because the other doesn't recognize them for who they are.

Director: Is that the key to forming true, lasting bonds? Mutual recognition?

Sage: Yes.

Director: But there's something I don't understand. How can a bond form with anything less than mutual recognition?

Sage: There might be recognition of parts but not the whole.

Director: So there are bonds of varying strength?

Sage: Yes. We're bonded more closely to some than others.

Director: Do bonds ever conflict?

Sage: You mean, if I'm bonded to one I can't be bonded to another?

Director: No, I was thinking you might be bonded to both but they're in tension.

Sage: Oh, that certainly happens.

Director: So what can you do?

Sage: Learn to live with tension — and let that help you grow.

~ Surrender (Artist, Director, Heir, Sage)

Heir: We must never surrender.

Director: Sage?

Sage: I think there are times when it's wise to surrender.

Artist: Such as?

Sage: When carrying on the fight is ruinous.

Heir: But what's more ruinous than surrender?

Sage: There are worse things in life.

Heir: I don't think so. What do you think, Director?

Director: Do you know the saying 'choose your battles'?

Heir: Of course. But not fighting and surrendering are two very different things.

Artist: But if you don't fight often enough haven't you surrendered in effect?

Heir: I suppose that's true.

Director: Well then, the question is: Do we sometimes choose not to fight, and make a sort of little surrender? Or do we always fight, and never, absolutely never, give in?

Artist: Give us an example.

Director: The four of us are going out to dinner. I want to go to restaurant X. You three want to go to restaurant Y. Do I refuse to give in, fight to the death, over restaurant X?

Heir: Of course not.

Director: So I give in. Or isn't that a good example?

Sage: No, I think it's a fine example. There are many little surrenders like this in life.

Director: How do we know when not to surrender?

Sage: We know when a principle is at stake.

Artist: Oh, there's always some sort of principle or other at stake. No, the time not to give in is when greater victory is at stake. Our victory in life.

~ Advantage (Artist, Director, Sage)

Artist: The wisest thing you can do is to serve your advantage.

Sage: Of course that's not true.

Artist: Then what's true wisdom, Sage? To serve the advantage of others?

Sage: It's not about advantage.

Artist: I know you like to say that, but in the end it is.

Sage: What an awful way to look at the world.

Director: What's a better way?

Sage: Not advantage, but harmony.

Artist: Harmony? Ha! You'd harmonize with those who try to take advantage of you?

Sage: Yes, if I could.

Director: Why?

Sage: Because then they'd stop trying to take advantage, and that serves my interest.

Artist: Your interest is to be at harmony with all?

Sage: Ultimately? Yes. As is yours.

Director: Sage, you seem to be distinguishing between interest and advantage.

Sage: I am.

Director: Tell us about the difference between the two.

Sage: Advantage is a zero sum matter. If I'm at an advantage, you're at a disadvantage. But interest is otherwise. My interest doesn't have to interfere with yours.

Artist: You sound like you've never heard of politics.

Sage: Politics doesn't have to be the way it is.

Director: Do you think Heir can make a difference here, through your advice?

Sage: Yes. And it's in all of our interest he does.

- Compassion (Artist, Director, Heir, Sage)

Sage: It's always wise to be compassionate.

Artist: Bah.

Heir: What's wrong, Artist?

Artist: Compassion is fine, Heir. But what's wise about it? Any fool can be compassionate.

Sage: There's nothing foolish about being compassionate.

Artist: And there's nothing wise about it, either.

Director: Who should be compassionate?

Artist: I think it's better to ask: Who shouldn't?

Heir: Well?

Sage: I think Artist is embarrassed to answer.

Artist: I'm not embarrassed. It's just an answer some of us won't like to hear.

Sage: You mean me.

Artist: Yes. Because the truth is that the wise should often resist compassion.

Sage: Why?

Artist: Because compassion can be quicksand. It sucks you in.

Sage: But that's ridiculous! I feel compassion all the time. And I never feel sucked in.

Artist: Maybe you don't know that you're sucked in. Or maybe....

Sage: Or maybe what? Oh, but forget about that. How would it be possible not to know I'm sucked in?

Artist: How? Who can say? The ways of the wise are mysterious. Even to themselves!

Heir: You two will never get anywhere together.

Artist: And you say that as if it just became clear.

~ Center (Artist, Director, Heir, Sage)

Heir: I want to be in the center of things.

Director: Why?

Heir: Because that's where all the action is!

Director: But it's also where all the trouble is, no?

Heir: Of course. There's no action without trouble. But listen to you! You're always in the center of things.

Director: How so?

Heir: You always talk to the most interesting people. Me included!

Director: There's trouble in talking to interesting people?

Heir: If you offend them there is.

Director: What do they do when offended?

Heir: Plot revenge.

Director: If I offended you, Sage, is that what you'd do?

Sage: No, of course not.

Director: Because the wise don't plot revenge?

Sage: That's right.

Artist: So what do they do?

Sage: They consider that only fools offend. And they rest content in that knowledge.

Director: Well, I'm in luck. I love to talk to the wise. And with them at worst I'm a fool!

Artist: But then why do you talk to me?

Director: Because you're wiser than you know.

Heir: But what about those who think they're wiser than they are?

Director: And they're in the center? Then our duty is to gently, but firmly, push them out.

~ Myth (Artist, Director, Heir, Sage)

Director: Do the wise deal in myths?

Sage: Traditional stories? Yes, Director, because these stories help illuminate certain truths.

Artist: Oh, I thought by 'myth' Director was talking about widely held false beliefs.

Sage: The wise do deal in those beliefs — in order to dispel them.

Director: Dispel them and offer nothing in return?

Sage: Of course not.

Heir: But what do the wise offer? The beliefs inherent to the traditional stories?

Sage: Not quite. The wise give something more. True beliefs of their own.

Artist: What's a true belief?

Sage: A belief that's good for you.

Heir: But as you've said, a belief that's good for you might not be good for someone else.

Director: Sage, tell us how a belief can be good for you and others, too.

Sage: It's very simple, really. Beliefs are good for those they uplift.

Artist: Beliefs uplift? How so?

Sage: They elevate those who hold them, elevate in a moral or spiritual sense.

Artist: And what does this elevation do?

Sage: Do? It inspires happiness and hope!

Heir: And there are examples of this inspiration in the traditional stories?

Sage: Of course there are — many.

Artist: So when you offer your true beliefs for sale, you rely on these tales for support?

Sage: Oh, Artist, count on you to see it that way. Belief is never for sale. It's beyond all price. And if you don't believe me — do I have a story for you.

~ Mockery (Artist, Director, Heir, Sage)

Sage: We mock what we don't understand.

Artist: 'We' might. But I mock what I understand all too well.

Sage: And what comes of your mockery?

Artist: Satisfaction.

Sage: Oh, I don't believe you. I think your mockery leaves a bad taste in your mouth.

Artist: Why do you say that? Because it leaves a bad taste in yours?

Sage: It's been many years since I've mocked.

Heir: I'm not one for mockery.

Director: Neither am I.

Sage: Mockery is a very selfish thing.

Artist: To the contrary. Mockery helps dispel false belief.

Heir: I don't know, Artist. People often hold on all the more tightly in response to mockery.

Artist: So how would you get rid of false belief? Through reason?

Heir: Yes. And example.

Artist: Example of what?

Sage: True belief. What else?

Director: Tell us. Does mockery ever touch true belief?

Sage: Not as much as the mocking one might think.

Artist: And why is that?

Sage: Because true belief, in response to mockery, sinks deeper into the soul.

Artist: Where it can never be found?

Sage: Oh, it can always be found — provided you know where to look.

~ Piety (Artist, Director, Heir, Sage)

Director: What are the pieties of our time?

Heir: It depends who you ask.

Director: What might one person say?

Heir: The individual. We revere the individual.

Sage: And another person might say we revere the community.

Heir: And a third might say we revere the individual in the community.

Director: But only when the individual fits in well?

Heir: Of course. Why revere someone who suffers from not fitting in?

Sage: Oh, but I think suffering, too, is one of our pieties.

Director: Because suffering is noble and worthy of reverence?

Sage: Yes.

Heir: But why do we think it's noble?

Artist: I know why. Because once we ennoble we don't have to do anything more.

Director: You mean we can then, with a good conscience, let the suffering suffer?

Artist: Yes.

Sage: But we also revere the relief of suffering.

Director: Is it more noble to relieve suffering than to suffer?

Sage: I think it is.

Heir: I tend to agree. But we're still saying we're pious toward those who suffer. So what happens when they find relief and suffer no more? Do they feel a loss of respect?

Director: Well, don't we also revere well-being?

Heir: I think we do. But now it seems we revere just about everything! And if we're pious towards all, aren't we pious... toward none?

~ Wine (Artist, Director, Heir, Sage)

Heir: Artist, what do you revere?

Artist: Me? Ha! Wine.

Heir: Fine wine or any old wine?

Artist: The finer the wine the more pious I am.

Director: But are you saying the more you drink the more reverent you become?

Artist: That's what happens with sad drunks. They grow too serious.

Heir: Are you a sad drunk? I've never really seen you get deep into your cups.

Artist: And you won't. Because the answer is yes. I grow sad.

Sage: Always?

Artist: Only when I have reason to be sad. But I often do.

Sage: But if you have reason to be sad, why aren't you sad when you're sober?

Artist: Because then the reasons aren't so clear.

Sage: Drinking makes reasons clear?

Artist: Sage, haven't you heard there's truth in wine?

Sage: Yes, but I thought that was only in relation to others.

Artist: Well, can't we be others to ourselves?

Heir: Of course we can. So, Artist, I'd like to introduce you to — yourself!

Artist: And why would you do that?

Director: Because he wants to help your sober self work your sadness through.

Heir: Exactly so.

Artist: But my sober self is proof enough against the sadness in my soul.

Heir: Then be more or less sober, and leave your saddened self alone — to shrivel... and die.

~ Awe (Artist, Director, Heir, Sage)

Artist: Wisdom should make us stand in awe.

Sage: Ha, ha. Why?

Artist: Why? Because wisdom is an awesome thing!

Sage: Are you in awe of me?

Artist: Ha! Of course not.

Sage: Because you think I'm not wise?

Artist: Yes. And it's because you take the easy way out.

Sage: The easy way? How so?

Artist: To be wise you have to understand your power and use it well. This is hard.

Sage: So you think I don't understand? Or do I not use my power very well?

Artist: Both.

Director: Tell us, Artist. Do we all have some power?

Artist: Yes, we do.

Director: And are you in awe if someone with very little power understands it and uses it to good effect?

Artist: I'm always in awe of beauty, yes.

Director: So there's no excuse for any of us?

Artist: No excuse at all.

Heir: Then why don't you cause awe in me?

Artist: Well, think about awe. Doesn't it involve a mixture of wonder and fear?

Heir: I suppose that's so. And I often wonder at you. But I wouldn't say I fear.

Artist: Exactly. And so I need to work on that. But the good news is that wonder is the harder part. Because with someone as sensitive as you, a touch of fear is all it takes.

~ Conflict (Artist, Director, Heir, Sage)

Sage: The wise foresee.

Artist: Foresee what?

Sage: Both good and bad.

Artist: And what do they do about what they see?

Sage: What else? Avoid the bad and seek the good.

Artist: But what's the bad? Conflict?

Sage: Why do you ask that?

Artist: Because I think conflict is good, or can lead to good. So somehow I knew you couldn't think that.

Heir: You think the wise avoid conflict?

Artist: As a rule? Yes.

Director: But then who seeks out conflict? The unwise?

Artist: No, the truly wise.

Heir: So you're suggesting you and Sage have opposite notions of wisdom.

Artist: Does that come as any surprise?

Heir: No, but which of you is right?

Director: To answer that it seems we have to say whether avoiding or seeking out conflict is best.

Heir: All I can say is sometimes I avoid it, and sometimes I seek it.

Director: How do you know when to do which?

Heir: I have to know what conflict is likely to bring.

Artist: And how do you know that?

Heir: I experiment.

~ Preparation (Artist, Director, Heir, Sage)

Heir: Sometimes you stumble into good. But mostly you have to prepare.

Artist: How do people know how to prepare? I mean, can't they have false opinions about what leads to good?

Sage: Of course they can. And then their preparations actually make good harder to achieve.

Director: So how can they correct their false opinions?

Heir: They can experiment.

Sage: And if experiment never shows the way?

Heir: Then they're doing something wrong.

Director: Yes, but if their experiments succeed?

Heir: Then they know how to prepare for what they want, and they'll have a greater good sooner than they otherwise would.

Director: I can see how preparation might make good better when it comes. But can being prepared really make it come sooner?

Heir: You mean good just comes when it comes, ready or not?

Director: That's what I'm wondering.

Heir: Well, Artist, what do you think?

Artist: I think we never know why good comes when it does. So all we can do is be prepared.

Heir: And when we are, then what should we do? Just wait and see?

Sage: Yes.

Heir: Oh, Sage, who has the patience for that?

Sage: Those who'd rather not force things, and scare the good away.

Heir: But why force — when we can woo?

~ Imparting (Director, Sage)

Director: Must the wise impart their wisdom to others?

Sage: Must they? That's a strong way of putting it.

Director: Let me put it this way. Could you take it if you never got to pass your wisdom on?

Sage: Well, honestly? No.

Director: And that's why you advise others?

Sage: It is. But what about you?

Director: I'm not wise.

Sage: Yes, but what about your philosophy?

Director: I don't have a philosophy.

Sage: Then what have you got?

Director: Philosophy itself.

Sage: Questioning and so on?

Director: And so on, yes.

Sage: And that's what you want to pass on?

Director: It is.

Sage: Why?

Director: Why do you want to pass your wisdom on?

Sage: So there's something of me that doesn't die. Is that how it is with you?

Director: It used to be, Sage.

Sage: Used to be?

Director: I don't believe I'll live on with philosophy.

Sage: Then I don't understand why you do what you do.

- Cheerfulness (Director, Heir)

Director: Heir, you've seen something of politics. So tell me. Does it make you cheerful?

Heir: Often it does. Does philosophy make you cheerful?

Director: Often times, yes. When does politics make you cheerful?

Heir: Oh, it's hard to explain.

Director: Meaning you don't know?

Heir: I know when I'm cheerful, but I can't always say precisely what makes me so. When does philosophy make you cheerful?

Director: When someone I encounter catches a glimpse of what philosophy is.

Heir: Only a glimpse?

Director: A glimpse is all it takes.

Heir: I think you're being lazy.

Director: Lazy?

Heir: Why not show them more, much more than a glimpse?

Director: Because once they've caught a glimpse they have to do it on their own.

Heir: I thought you didn't 'do' philosophy.

Director: 'Do' for lack of a better term. And you see? We start talking about philosophy and already we're having trouble with words.

Heir: So you're cheered by starting trouble then leaving it to others?

Director: Well, when you put it that way....

Heir: Yes, but I don't believe you have bad intent. I believe you have just as much trouble as those you encounter.

Director: Thanks. But why don't you have trouble? You and I have had many encounters.

Heir: Because I have the antidote to your kind of trouble, my friend. Politics.

- Change (Director, Heir, Sage)

Sage: The wise know when to stay firm and when to change.

Heir: I think you're confusing things, Sage.

Sage: How so?

Heir: Staying firm, being solid, is the opposite of being fluid, isn't it?

Sage: Yes, of course.

Heir: And change is fluid?

Sage: Certainly.

Heir: So here's what I want to know. What if you're always fluid?

Director: Like you?

Heir: Yes like me.

Sage: You're always changing? But if you're always changing isn't the only real change to stop?

Heir: Exactly. But why would you ever want to freeze yourself up like that? So you should say this: The wise know to flow.

Director: Hmm, yes. But there's one thing I wonder, Heir. The people you'll represent — are they fluid like you, or are they more solid?

Heir: Well, yes, of course — they're more solid. But that doesn't change the truth of what I said about the wise.

Director: Yes, my friend. But tell me something you'd know better than I. Does like vote for like, or does like vote for unlike?

Heir: Like tends to vote for like — but not always.

Director: No, certainly not always. But if you still hope to be elected, won't you have to appear, at least to some degree, solid? And if you appear to be solid, won't you actually be solid? Do we need to get into this in detail, or do you see what I mean?

Sage: I think he sees, Director. And I think there's some truth in what he said about flow. But now I think he sees there's some truth in what I said, too.

~ Works (Artist, Director, Heir, Sage)

Sage: It's not enough to be wise. You have to perform works of wisdom, too.

Artist: Give us an example of a work of wisdom.

Sage: A smile at just the right time.

Artist: Ha! And what does that smile mean?

Sage: Whatever is called for at the moment.

Artist: Ah, an all-purpose smile. The ultimate work of wisdom.

Heir: Oh, Artist. What did you expect? You know it's hard to describe a work of wisdom in so many words. But I wonder about philosophy.

Director: What do you wonder?

Heir: Can it describe its works in so many words?

Director: Yes. But there's only one work. Conversation. It can be conversation in person or through books, many and various types of books. But philosophers must converse.

Artist: You're letting yourself off pretty easily, aren't you?

Sage: But if Director is let off easily, so am I.

Heir: Why do you say that?

Sage: Because the main work of the wise also is conversation.

Director: Yes, I believe it's true. And you, Heir, are in the same boat.

Heir: Politics is conversation? Don't tell me. I converse with the electorate while I campaign. And then I converse with them when I'm in office. And I converse with my peers in the work of the legislature. Conversation, conversation, conversation.

Director: I'm glad you agree. And you, Artist, you're in conversation with your audience, aren't you?

Artist: Well, yes. But out of all this conversation, which type is best?

Heir: Oh, but do you really want to compete? No, let's just say we're equals in this. And if one of us seems to pull ahead of the others, let's promise we'll never say.

~ Reflection (Artist, Sage)

Sage: Reflection is a turning inward.

Artist: So extroverts don't reflect?

Sage: Of course they do. But they don't dwell on their reflections.

Artist: And that's what you think introverts do? Dwell on them?

Sage: Don't you think it's true?

Artist: I don't know. I'm something of a combination of introvert and extrovert. And I can't tell which part dwells on what.

Sage: But what else is there to dwell on but thoughts? And who dwells on thoughts but introverts?

Artist: Yes, but what about feelings?

Sage: Thoughts, feelings — what's the difference?

Artist: What? Don't you know that feelings can shape thoughts, and thoughts can shape feelings? If they weren't two very different things, they couldn't have such an influence on each other.

Sage: So which is better to dwell upon? Thoughts or feelings?

Artist: Neither.

Sage: Then let me rephrase. Which is better to reflect upon?

Artist: Both, assuming by 'reflect' we mean to think.

Sage: So we think about our feelings. But what does it mean to think about our thoughts?

Artist: We reflect upon the quality of our thoughts.

Sage: And what makes for a high quality thought?

Artist: Fidelity to the initial reaction, the reaction that led to thought.

Sage: You surprise me, Artist. Who would have guessed you'd reduce thought to a matter of keeping faith?

~ Imitation (Artist, Sage)

Artist: Can we successfully imitate wisdom?

Sage: I'm not sure I understand what you're asking.

Artist: I'm asking if wisdom is uniquely your own.

Sage: Yes and no.

Artist: How so?

Sage: Each person must be wise in their own way. But they might not know wisdom is possible unless they learn from others who are wise.

Artist: And what do they learn from these others? Wisdom in general but not in particular, the particulars that will go into being wise in their own way?

Sage: Yes. And isn't that how it is with art?

Artist: Bad artists imitate particulars. But good artists imitate the gist of good art.

Sage: And what's the gist of good art?

Artist: The truth about life.

Sage: Interesting! That's the gist of wisdom, too.

Artist: Yes, but you can't really say my art and your wisdom are anything alike.

Sage: Why not?

Artist: At times my art gets dark. You can't tell me your wisdom gets dark.

Sage: But what if I say my dark wisdom is wisdom you can't see?

Artist: You can say it but I won't believe you have it.

Sage: Well, I'll just take that as a compliment!

Artist: But it's meant more as an insult. Life has both light and dark. That's its truth.

Sage: So you're saying I'm only halfway wise? That I need to imitate your work?

Artist: Worse. Halfway wise is nothing wise, just as halfway truth is lies. So imitate me all you want — you still need to come to life on your own.

- Firmness (Heir, Sage)

Heir: Oh, you just have to be firm with Artist.

Sage: But he can be so... mean.

Heir: You don't think he was serious about halfway wise and so on, do you?

Sage: I think he was very serious.

Heir: But do you believe it's true?

Sage: I don't know. What if I really am only halfway wise? Or what if I'm three quarters wise? Or nine tenths? Isn't it all the same?

Heir: Sage, do you really think ninety-nine hundredths wise is the same as halfway wise?

Sage: I don't know.

Heir: Well that's ridiculous. Artist is causing you to lose your nerve.

Sage: But why do I need nerve in order to be wise? Doesn't the need for nerve suggest I'm not wholly wise?

Heir: But who in the world is wholly wise?

Sage: Well, you have a point.

Heir: Is Artist wholly wise? Him and his truth about life?

Sage: I don't believe he is.

Heir: And what about you? Are you wholly wise?

Sage: I'm glad you're being firm with me. The answer is no.

Heir: So take whatever wisdom you've got and make the most of it. Right?

Sage: Right. But what if my wisdom is less than half?

Heir: Sage! I know your wisdom is more than half.

Sage: How do you know?

Heir: Because you're at least as wise as I am — and there's no way I'm less than half!

~ Failure (Artist, Director, Sage)

Artist: How many mistakes does it take to fail?

Sage: Fail at what?

Artist: Life.

Sage: I don't think you can put a number on it.

Artist: But you can put a percentage on it. So, what if more than half of what you do is a mistake? Failure?

Sage: No, I don't believe it's failure. What if you make ninety-nine mistakes and the hundredth time is a resounding success?

Artist: The failures will drown out the success.

Sage: I don't believe that's true.

Director: Why not?

Sage: Because, Director, success in this world is rare. And the rare outshines the common.

Director: But what about those who have repeated success? You do think such success is possible, don't you?

Sage: Well, yes.

Director: So if I succeed ninety-nine times, and the hundredth I fail — does the rare failure eclipse the common success?

Sage: No, of course not.

Artist: Why not?

Sage: It's as I said, success in this world is rare — even if there are those who almost always succeed.

Artist: What would it take for people like that to fail?

Sage: They would have to somehow lose their way.

Director: I'd put it differently, Sage. They fail when they stop trying to find their way.

~ Assumptions (Artist, Director, Heir, Sage)

Sage: The wise never assume.

Heir: Neither do philosophers.

Director: Neither do true leaders.

Artist: Neither do true artists.

Sage: Why do some of us require a 'true' and others don't?

Artist: Ha! Could it be because wisdom and philosophy are vain?

Heir: And leaders and artists aren't?

Artist: Oh, I'm just teasing. We're all vain and deserve a 'true'.

Director: I'm not so sure it's vanity that calls for that qualification.

Sage: Then what does?

Director: The simple fact that all of us make assumptions from time to time.

Heir: And we're only true when we don't? I think that makes sense.

Artist: But what about the times when we should assume?

Sage: Should assume? We should never assume.

Artist: Why not?

Sage: Why not? Because when we assume we make mistakes!

Artist: Yes, but there are mistakes, and then there are mistakes.

Sage: Are you talking about your intentional mistakes?

Artist: Of course!

Sage: But we said an intentional mistake is a lie. Can we lie and be true?

Artist: Aren't there times when we have to lie? To a tyrant, for instance, in self-defense? And if we do what we must, aren't we true to ourselves?

Sage: So we can be true when we're false? My, what an assumption that is.

~ Arrogance (Director, Heir, Sage)

Sage: The wise are never arrogant.

Director: Why not?

Sage: Because in order to be wise you have to have an accurate sense of your own abilities and importance. That precludes arrogance.

Heir: But what if you think you're more able and important than others?

Director: Is that what you think about yourself?

Heir: I believe I'm more able. In fact, I know I'm more able. But I get hung up on the notion of importance.

Director: Why?

Heir: Because we believe those who think they're more important than others are not only arrogant but simply wrong.

Director: Because everyone is equally important?

Heir: Yes, and if I can put it crudely — a vote is a vote.

Director: Do you believe if our political system were different not everyone would be considered equally important?

Heir: You mean, for instance, if some people had ten votes and others only one? Yes, I suppose not everyone would be considered equally important.

Sage: But what about things other than votes?

Heir: What other things?

Sage: Money. Does having money make you more important?

Heir: I don't know, Sage. I think some people think it does. But I'm more inclined to wonder about those with more wisdom than others. More important?

Sage: It's hard to say.

Director: Why?

Sage: Because... it's hard to say.

~ Boundaries (Artist, Director, Heir, Sage)

Sage: The wise respect others' boundaries.

Heir: Why?

Sage: Because if we don't respect theirs, they won't respect ours.

Heir: What boundaries do I need?

Sage: We all need boundaries, Heir.

Heir: Director, do you have boundaries?

Director: When it comes to philosophy? No.

Artist: Ha! I knew he'd say that. But what about when it doesn't come to philosophy?

Director: When doesn't it come to philosophy?

Sage: When it comes to your personal matters.

Director: Well, yes — my personal matters aren't always appropriate for discussion.

Sage: So you do have boundaries.

Director: Yes, but I sometimes let others into my personal space.

Heir: So your boundaries shift, depending on who you're talking to — right?

Director: On who I'm talking to, Heir — yes. But circumstances also matter here.

Sage: And what sort of circumstances conduce to sharing your space?

Director: When I have something personal a friend needs to know.

Sage: Can you give us an example?

Director: My experience with philosophy.

Heir: It's really all about philosophy with you, both outside your personal space and within — isn't it?

Sage: But what knowledge of his experience with philosophy does anyone need? We can all get our own experience by reading books, by going to lectures, by talking to philosophers whose boundaries we respect. So, Director, I simply fail to see your point.

~ Depths and Heights (Artist, Director, Sage)

Artist: Of course we must strive to scale the heights.

Sage: And when we've scaled we must dive down into the depths.

Artist: But why?

Sage: So we aren't ruined by the heights.

Artist: How do the heights ruin us?

Sage: Through rarified air.

Artist: And the depths counter that through the great pressure we feel as we sink?

Sage: Naturally. And if the pressure grows too great, we can rise and climb once more.

Artist: So we go down and up and up and down?

Sage: Don't we? Or do we stay at sea level all of our lives?

Artist: Director, what do you think?

Director: I'm wondering why Sage thinks rarified air can ruin us.

Sage: It's because we need a good dose of pressure in our lives.

Artist: Why?

Sage: Because pressure motivates.

Artist: But too much pressure can have the opposite effect.

Sage: And that's why I said we can rise and climb when the pressure grows too great.

Director: Tell me, Sage. Do you think some are born to the heights?

Sage: Yes, of course.

Director: And is it hard to induce them to go down into the depths?

Sage: Very hard at times.

Director: Why do you think that is?

Sage: Because who likes pressure when they're accustomed to none?

~ Heights and Depths (Artist, Director, Sage)

Artist: But is there really no pressure on high?

Director: You think our metaphor is wrong?

Artist: Like most metaphors, yes.

Director: So tell us how it really is.

Artist: Alright. When you're on high what do you have?

Director: A commanding view.

Artist: Yes, Director. And when you have a commanding view, what do you think you want to do?

Director: I suppose you want to command.

Artist: Exactly. And when you command what do you feel?

Director: You feel pressure.

Artist: Of course. And where do you find pressure?

Director: Not in the heights?

Artist: That's right. You find pressure in the depths.

Director: In our metaphor, at least.

Artist: Yes, yes. And that's the point. That's why the metaphor is no good. Don't you agree?

Sage: But the metaphor would be fine if the commander came down from on high in order to command. Wouldn't it?

Artist: But then the commander loses the commanding view.

Sage: Maybe the commander just has to remember what he or she saw.

Artist: You'd trust memory over vision?

Sage: Yes, Artist, if I had no other choice. But in that case I'd like the commander to refresh that memory, as often as he or she can.

- Gifts (Artist, Director, Heir, Sage)

Heir: Would I be satisfied if people looked up to me? No, of course not.

Director: Why? Don't you want people to look up to you?

Heir: I want them to look at me for what I am. And to do that they need to look down.

Sage: What are you talking about?

Heir: Have you ever been to a large sports arena to watch a game?

Sage: I have.

Heir: Weren't you looking down at the players on the field?

Sage: Well, yes. But you shouldn't be so literal about it.

Heir: Why not? Aren't I stepping onto a sort of playing field? Don't I want people to watch me play?

Artist: Yes, you're making good sense. And you're looking for twofold satisfaction.

Heir: Yes, Artist. But tell me how so.

Artist: You want the satisfaction of playing well, very well. And you want the satisfaction of great applause.

Heir: Yes!

Director: So you have to know the game.

Heir: But it's not enough to know the game. You have to be able to play it.

Director: What does it take to be able to play it?

Heir: Natural gifts enhanced by training.

Director: I don't deny you have the gifts. But what training have you got?

Heir: Oh, I'll get that in the election and my first term.

Sage: You'll be going up against players with much more knowledge and training, you know.

Heir: Yes, but that only goes so far — when you haven't got the gifts.

- Giving (Artist, Director, Heir)

Director: Tell me, Heir. When you give a gift, do you give it to someone?

Heir: Of course.

Director: Who do you give it to?

Heir: Someone I want to give it to.

Director: Do you know this person? Or do you give the gift to someone you don't know?

Heir: Yes, I know what you're driving at. Why give the greatest gift I can give, myself, to the people — people I don't know?

Director: Well?

Heir: But I know them, Director.

Director: Know them each individually?

Heir: Of course not. And I'm not giving myself to them each individually.

Director: You're not?

Heir: I'm giving myself to them as the people.

Director: I'm not sure I understood that grammar. Are you saying you're giving yourself as the people?

Heir: You really can be ridiculous sometimes. I'm giving myself to the people.

Director: Why?

Heir: Artist, you give your work to the people. Tell him why we give.

Artist: I give my work to the people who are interested in my work. That's all.

Heir: Well, then the difference is that most everyone is interested in my work.

Director: Then will most everyone be grateful for your gift? Or doesn't that matter?

Heir: Doesn't it matter? Of course it matters! And it takes just the right gift for gratitude.

Director: Then to give just the right gift, I suppose you'll have to make a study of the people's tastes, and become what they want. Or isn't that what you're after?

- Ignorance (Director, Sage)

Director: I set it down to ignorance.

Sage: You mean he doesn't know what he has to give?

Director: Yes. And maybe it's the whole notion of giving that's the problem here.

Sage: If not as giving, then how should he think about his service to the community?

Director: Maybe it's a matter of taking.

Sage: Taking what?

Director: Taking their votes. Taking their interest and attention. Taking their support. And then taking their applause.

Sage: But they want to be given something in return for all that.

Director: Can't he give them victory? That's something he can share with them without losing it for himself. No?

Sage: Yes. But what if Artist is right? What if victory for them isn't victory for us?

Director: What's this? Us versus them? But who is 'us'?

Sage: People like you and me.

Director: I don't know....

Sage: What's wrong?

Director: I'm ignorant as to whether you and I, and people who might seem like, constitute an 'us'.

Sage: You're talking in political terms?

Director: Yes, of course. What else are we talking about but political things?

Sage: Okay. But I'm just saying victory is never victory for all. Even if Heir wins, we might miss out.

Director: Miss out? On what?

Sage: If you honestly don't know, I won't be the one to say.

~ Choice (Director, Sage)

Sage: But, Director, sometimes we have no choice. There are political forces greater than us.

Director: Do you think everyone feels that way?

Sage: Yes, I do.

Director: So no one person always feels greater than any given force?

Sage: What? Of course not.

Director: Not even Heir?

Sage: Well, that's the problem. I sometimes think he does. Or rather, he thinks he can ride the political forces like a wave.

Director: So the choice, as he sees it, is simply which wave to catch, then how best to ride?

Sage: I think that's exactly so.

Director: But isn't that all anyone in politics can do?

Sage: I suppose it is, at times.

Director: Hmm. Tell me. How are political forces created?

Sage: They're basically forces of nature.

Director: Isn't the object of science and technology to understand and harness nature?

Sage: True. But what are you saying? That it's possible to understand and harness political force?

Director: Isn't that what great leaders do?

Sage: It's what they seem to do. Riding the wave, the leader appears to command where it goes.

Director: So why do people choose to believe that's true, that the leader commands?

Sage: They fear the wave.

~ Seeds (Artist, Director, Heir)

Heir: But why do we have to think about politics as waves? Why can't it be earth, working the earth?

Artist: What do you mean?

Heir: Earth that we plow and seeds that we sow for the sake of a great harvest. That's politics.

Artist: Yes, that sounds nice. And I know we talked about soil on the hands being what voters want to see. But....

Director: What kind of seeds would you plant?

Heir: Oh, Director. It's just a metaphor.

Director: Then let me ask. What kind of laws would you promulgate?

Heir: It's not that simple.

Director: What? Not simple?

Heir: You know it's not. I have to size things up before I can say.

Director: You mean you have to know who supports what?

Heir: Of course. That's how you get things done.

Director: But you're not the only one trying to get things done.

Heir: Everyone is trying to get things done.

Director: So in the lawmaking process, your peers, they'll try to size you up?

Heir: You know they will.

Director: They'll ask you what laws you support? What seeds you'd sow?

Heir: Yes, but it's more complicated than that. What I say I support depends on what others support. And it's that way with all the other legislators, too.

Director: Do the voters understand how complex all this is?

Heir: Some of them do. But 'some' aren't enough to win.

~ Observation (Artist, Director, Heir, Sage)

Artist: I'd love to watch politics in the making.

Heir: Run for office.

Artist: No, I mean I'd like to observe for an afternoon.

Sage: You think that would be enough?

Artist: How difficult to understand can it be?

Heir: I don't think there's anything as difficult to understand as politics.

Artist: It takes a real genius to master it?

Heir: Honestly? Yes.

Artist: Well, I'd love to observe the master at work.

Heir: But it's not fair.

Artist: Why not?

Heir: You'd get to watch me, but I wouldn't get to watch you!

Director: I'm sure Artist wouldn't mind a fair trade. An afternoon with you for an afternoon with him.

Artist: But what's he going to watch? Me typing on a keyboard, sketching on a pad?

Heir: I want to watch your process as you generate ideas.

Artist: Ideas? Ha! You'd have to be witness to my whole life.

Heir: Then write me something about your life. Something that takes you an afternoon to do. And then I'll make the trade.

Director: That sounds fair to me.

Artist: But it doesn't sound fair to me. What if I'm trading gold for coal?

Heir: Coal that you can make into diamonds with your art!

Artist: Oh, Heir, that's just a myth. Diamonds aren't formed from coal. But I'll give you credit. You're a master. But of what I'd rather not say.

- Healing (Artist, Director, Heir, Sage)

Sage: Wisdom heals. It's a balm for the soul.

Artist: Beautiful art heals, too, you know.

Director: You two seem to be finding more and more in common.

Heir: But what have you got in common with them? Does philosophy heal?

Director: Philosophy is the ultimate medicine. But it calls for the greatest health and strength, in both the philosopher and the one to be healed.

Heir: But if you have health and strength why be healed?

Director: Because health and strength can be under constant attack.

Heir: And it's philosophy's job to join the fight?

Director: It's philosophy's job to teach you how to fight, to keep yourself at full strength.

Heir: And when you win the fight you're healed?

Artist: Yes, yes — of course. But politics, too, is medicine like this, only in a higher way. Do you know what it heals?

Heir: The soul of the people.

Artist: Yes! And do you know what it takes to heal the soul of the people?

Heir: The greatest health and strength, in leader and people both.

Sage: Artist, listen to you leading Heir on to wisdom!

Director: Oh, he's just flattering himself. Tell us, Artist. How does beautiful art differ from politics?

Artist: Well, yes, I think of art as the equal of politics — the highest healing there is... even though it's not for all.

Heir: So art is more exclusive than politics?

Artist: Ha! Don't pretend to be offended with me. Save that for Director and Sage. They attempt to heal only one at a time. And what's more exclusive than that?

~ Knots (Artist, Director, Heir, Sage)

Sage: Yes, but I heal one, and another, and another — and it all adds up. And I think it's the same with philosophy. But I'd like to learn how it heals.

Heir: To see how philosophy heals we need someone who's sick. But we three are a mostly healthy lot.

Sage: Then let's find someone who's sick. Or does it take a certain sort of sick person, one philosophically inclined?

Artist: Philosophically inclined? But how do we know the inclination? A love of philosophical books? A love of talking the way Director talks?

Director: You're right to speak of love. But philosophy's love can be difficult to recognize and hard to understand.

Sage: Oh, it can't be that hard. It's the love of wisdom, right? So what's the first step?

Director: In the healing process? A simple theoretical examination.

Heir: Theoretical? Why?

Director: Because we need to know what our patient thinks about certain things.

Artist: If the patient does in fact think.

Director: A fair point. No thinking, no help from philosophy.

Artist: Yes, and then someone like Sage might be better suited to help. Ha!

Director: Now, if our investigation turns up knots, we have to decide what to do.

Heir: Knots? Like the Gordian knot?

Director: Yes. When under attack people often knot themselves up. We can leave the knots alone, try to work them free, or cut them in half with a sharp enough blade.

Heir: What's the best thing to do?

Director: Well, assuming we don't want to leave them alone, we might exercise patience and skill to help work the knots through. In that case, the person is free and will know a thing or two about knots. But if we cut, the person is free in no time at all — but will almost certainly be left hanging, at least for a while, at loose ends.

~ Success (Artist, Director, Heir, Sage)

Heir: Yes, but we're not getting the whole story.

Director: What's the whole story, Heir?

Heir: That removing the knot can prove fatal.

Sage: Fatal? How?

Heir: Some people just can't seem to live without knots.

Artist: Ha! So if you're unsure what kind of person you're dealing with, what must you do?

Sage: I'll tell you what you must do. Slowly work the knot through. Build the person's confidence up as you go. And if he or she is too uneasy, you tie the knot up a little again. Two steps forward, one step back.

Artist: That would take the patience of a saint. And I can see you take that as a compliment! But do you know my opinion?

Heir: I think I do. Cut the knot and let all be damned.

Artist: Yes.

Sage: And what happens then? It's either death or hanging at loose ends? So let's say you succeed, and the people whose knots you cut are in the latter state. Do you really want to populate the world with people like that?

Artist: Yes, yes. Then why don't you teach them to tie their own knots back up again, if you must? And then teach them to untie them. And to tie them again.

Sage: Command of your own knot! I'd call that success.

Artist: Oh, don't get carried away. Command of your knot is merely a crutch. True success involves no knots.

Director: Do you think many mistake command for success?

Artist: I do. But often enough they don't even command. They hide in their knot.

Heir: And what do they hide themselves from? Attack?

Artist: Yes, but not so much as from knowledge of others' success.

~ Mastery (Artist, Sage)

Artist: Master of Knots. That's what I think they'll call you. Ha!

Sage: And why do you punctuate your compliment with a laugh?

Artist: Sorry, it's just a habit.

Sage: A habit you make no effort to master?

Artist: I'd try to master it if I thought it were somehow wrong.

Sage: Well, it makes people uneasy.

Artist: But unease isn't necessarily bad. Maybe I'm the Master of Unease, to complement your being Master of Knots.

Sage: And how are those things complementary?

Artist: I'll make them feel uneasy, and you...

Sage: ...can knot them up?

Artist: Yes! And wouldn't that be fine? We'll take turns. You make them feel safe, and I'll show them how things really stand when you hand them off to me.

Sage: But, Artist, why would I want to hand them off to you, to make them to feel anxious?

Artist: How else do you expect them to learn, to grow? Or isn't growth part of your wisdom?

Sage: Certainly growth is part. But can't we grow without unease?

Artist: Growth is always outside our comfort zone. And so we feel unease.

Sage: But what about the poor souls who are always uneasy, always anxious?

Artist: Wouldn't you agree they have the greatest potential to grow, the most to master?

Sage: As if by some divine justice?

Artist: I wouldn't go that far.

Sage: But I would. And I think that's just what they need to hear.

- Light (Artist, Director, Heir, Sage)

Artist: Look! The color of dawn! The party will soon be over.

Heir: And yet Director hardly looks drunk.

Director: You seem to be holding up rather well yourself. But Artist seems a little wobbly. And Sage seems tipsy at best. I guess we forgot to keep up.

Sage: Somehow I don't think you forgot. You have a higher tolerance, is all.

Director: And what's Heir's tolerance? Will he be a tolerant leader?

Heir: Tolerant of what?

Director: Philosophy.

Sage: Does he have reason not to be tolerant of philosophy?

Director: I don't know.

Sage: You know, Director, you make us suspicious of philosophy when you answer like that.

Director: How should I answer?

Sage: You should say you'll be a firm supporter of Heir.

Director: I plan to be. Though I'm not so sure my support will do much good.

Heir: Why not?

Director: You're at a point, Heir, where the real good you need must come from yourself.

Heir: In an election? And what will this good from myself bring? Victory?

Director: Yes, there's that. But you want greatness, and not just middling success.

Sage: Greatness requires you go it alone?

Director: Yes, Sage. But, oh, Heir needs his friends, and that's wonderful. But, in the end, he must walk his way apart — even when surrounded by friends.

Heir: Walk my way into destiny? Together and alone at once?

Director: Yes. And look! The sun has come up! Now let's see if your sun, too — can rise.

~ Darkness (Director, Sage)

Sage: I'm surprised you told Heir he must go it alone.

Director: You don't think it's true?

Sage: It just seems so cold.

Director: Cold even though we'll be there with him?

Sage: Yes!

Director: Why?

Sage: Because you're telling him to put up a barrier.

Director: Don't you think he needs some protection from political life?

Sage: Of course. But not from his friends!

Director: You'd travel with him without a barrier?

Sage: No doubt I would.

Director: But what if he travels in the dark?

Sage: What are you talking about?

Director: If you travel with him in the dark, and he has no barrier — might you not stumble into him and do him harm?

Sage: You're talking crazy, Director.

Director: Am I? You don't think he'll have to work day and night to win his race?

Sage: Yes, of course he will.

Director: And might night not come, at times, in the full light of day? Do you understand what I mean?

Sage: Oh, I understand. And that's what I don't like!

Director: But what about Heir? Do you think he'll enjoy his daytime night?

Sage: I think he very well might. And that's exactly why we can't let him go it alone.

~ Rule (Artist, Director, Heir, Sage)

Sage: Rule? Who talks about rule anymore? But there's no reason why we can't. And I'll say this. Good rule, proper rule, is a matter of knowledge.

Artist: Ha! I don't buy that for a minute.

Sage: Why not?

Artist: Because good rule is all about power. If I take a bad ruler, and hold a gun to their head, and say, 'Rule well, you fool. Rule well or die!' What do you think happens?

Sage: Nothing, or worse — unless someone who knows tells them what to do each step along the way.

Artist: Yes, sure, tell them all you want — even so that they come to know. But if they don't have the power to act, what good does it do?

Director: And that's because knowledge isn't power?

Artist: Right. Power is power. And the bad rulers lack the power to rule well.

Director: Are you saying they'd rule well if they could?

Artist: Everyone would rule well if they could.

Sage: Now who's being ridiculous?

Artist: Laugh all you want. But it takes more power to rule well than badly.

Sage: But tyrants can be very powerful, sometimes much more so than leaders who rule well.

Artist: Tyrants often seem that way because they're compelled to seem that way, to seem as powerful as they can — because they fear for their own lives.

Director: And leaders who rule well generally don't?

Artist: Yes.

Sage: But is it possible to fear for your life and still rule well?

Heir: Certainly, Sage. And in that case the difference lies in knowing how to deal reasonably with your fear.

~ Beauty (Artist, Director, Heir, Sage)

Heir: Power is beautiful.

Sage: Naked power?

Heir: All power.

Sage: Even when put to bad use?

Heir: The bad use is ugly. But the power itself is beautiful.

Artist: I think Heir is finally drunk!

Heir: No, I'm perfectly within my senses. Think of fire. Fire is beautiful. The greater the fire the more beautiful, if you ask me. But, yes, fire destroys when not properly contained.

Director: So power must be properly contained. But how?

Heir: Through the democratic process, how else?

Artist: Why do we have to say 'democratic process'? Doesn't everyone know we don't have a strict, classical, direct democracy? We don't choose any office holders by lots. We don't vote directly on legislation and executive acts.

Sage: Yes, Artist, but for all its faults, we have the best and most beautiful system there is.

Artist: That may be. But isn't there a way to make it better and more beautiful?

Heir: Of course. By giving more power to the people.

Director: You mean more power to those who give their power to you.

Heir: Yes.

Artist: Ha!

Sage: And how will that power be contained?

Heir: My power? I'll limit myself to putting it only to good use. And the people will approve.

Artist: Then how much depends on what you, and the people, think is good.

~ Desperation (Artist, Director, Heir, Sage)

Sage: The wise are never desperate.

Artist: Oh, that's ridiculous. Never?

Sage: Never. But if we were talking about before they grew wise....

Artist: Ha! Let me guess. In that time before, it was their very desperation that helped them grow wise.

Sage: Yes, often enough — in the overcoming of it.

Director: Let's clarify something. What does it mean to be desperate?

Sage: To feel such hopelessness about a situation that you can't begin to deal with it.

Director: What makes the wise feel hope?

Sage: Knowing they can deal.

Director: But how can they know that?

Sage: By having no fear of failure.

Heir: That's interesting. That's how I feel about all the things I try to do.

Artist: You believe you'll succeed?

Heir: Not always. But I never fear for long I won't.

Director: Would you say most people fear failure?

Heir: Yes. And some of them grow desperate because they do. They're so afraid they can't even imagine how to deal, even though they know dealing is the key.

Director: So, Sage, what do you say to someone like that?

Sage: What can you say? Those who can't deal will fail.

Heir: Yes, but by failing they might learn that failure isn't so bad.

Director: Is failure really not that bad?

Heir: I wouldn't know.

~ Standards (Artist, Director, Heir, Sage)

Artist: Suppose someone fails but doesn't learn failure isn't so bad. What then?

Sage: They can't get over their fear of failure? Then they'll never be wise.

Director: Yes. But tell me, Sage. Is there an exception? A failure it's always wise to fear?

Sage: Well, of course. Failure to become yourself.

Director: You mean something like reaching your potential?

Sage: In a sense. But there's an important qualification.

Heir: What qualification? We either reach it or we don't.

Sage: Yes, but what standards do we use to measure what we achieve?

Heir: What do you mean?

Sage: Where do they come from? Outside of us, or inside?

Artist: Yes, yes. We should look to ourselves. But tell me, and tell me true. Don't you think we need standards from outside, too?

Sage: Why would we?

Artist: Why? Why, because we have to live in the world! Surely that's what you think.

Sage: I think those who enslave themselves to external standards are afraid, afraid their own internal standards aren't good enough.

Heir: We must never fear to live by our own standards and measure our success according to them?

Sage: Yes.

Director: But how do we know if a standard is truly our own? Can't we get confused?

Sage: We can. But we know our own standards because they're the ones we most fear.

Artist: Ha! I think you're on to something, Sage.

Heir: Because you once feared your very own standards and conquered that fear?

Artist: No, it's because I'm all too aware of the temptation — to run away from my fear.

~ Fame (Artist, Director, Sage)

Artist: I'm telling you. Fame can be a good way to know yourself.

Sage: But how could you possibly think that?

Artist: Fame is like a gigantic mirror, distorted at times, it's true — but a mirror nonetheless.

Director: What do you do with the distortions?

Artist: You let them spur you on to hunt for the truth about how you truly look.

Director: And that's so with both flattering and unflattering distortions?

Artist: Well, that's the thing. The unflattering will impel you to search for truth. If they don't cripple you, that is.

Director: How would they cripple you?

Artist: By overwhelming you. They leave you paralyzed.

Director: And how long do you stay in such a state?

Artist: Some stay all their lives.

Director: Do you worry about this for Heir?

Artist: Heir? No, he'll see so many flattering distortions I don't think the unflattering will ever overwhelm him.

Sage: You say that as if you're certain he'll have the unflattering.

Artist: Certain? Of course I'm certain! He'll have plenty of enemies, and they'll figure out exactly where he's weak.

Director: Would it be better for him not to be famous, to spare himself all that?

Artist: That's like telling the bull not to charge the red cape.

Director: But he's more matador than bull. No?

Artist: Well, you have a point. And that's fine. Usually the bulls don't do so well. But often enough they gore.

~ Virtue (Heir, Sage)

Sage: You need to be virtuous, Heir.

Heir: Why?

Sage: So people will admire you!

Heir: Ha, ha! Is that the only reason? I thought you were going to tell me I should be virtuous for me.

Sage: Well, you should.

Heir: Virtue is good for you and me and everyone else involved!

Sage: Please don't make it into a song.

Heir: Oh, Sage. I value your wisdom. You know that, don't you? You've given me some very good advice. But I think I'm right to make virtue into a song.

Sage: You just want the voters to sing along.

Heir: I want them all to sing along! Don't you realize how I look at this?

Sage: Of course I do. You don't want a majority of the votes. You want them all.

Heir: And what's wrong with that?

Sage: Nothing, if they're voting for your virtue and not some silly song.

Heir: I take it as an affront for a single vote to go the other way. So if a majority votes for me for my virtue, I'm happy — but I'm not satisfied.

Sage: And the only way to win the rest is through song and dance?

Heir: Dance! Ah, that's the thing. Dance! And when I've won, what other performers will be with me on the stage? Only the best dancers will do!

Sage: But you don't need performers.

Heir: What do I need? Doers? Doers can dance while they do. And whistle, too!

Sage: Alright. You've made your point.

Heir: The doers must dance to a virtuous tune! And I know what to have them... do.

~ Caution (Artist, Director, Sage)

Artist: They say there can be method to madness. But can there be method to wisdom?

Sage: Of course there can.

Artist: What sort of method?

Sage: It's hard to explain.

Artist: Why? Because it varies from wise person to wise person, or because it varies per case each wise person encounters?

Sage: It really doesn't vary much. Generally, the wise all have the same method for each encounter.

Director: That's funny. I would have thought the method varies.

Sage: Why do you say that?

Director: Well, look at it this way. Do you use the same method when approaching a rabid dog as you do a purring cat?

Sage: Yes, you approach each with caution.

Artist: Why the cat with caution? And why approach the dog at all?

Sage: You don't want to disturb the cat. And as for the dog, what can I say but that it wasn't my example?

Director: But now you make me wonder. Maybe we should all use the same method for everything. Caution.

Artist: But caution isn't really a method. It's more of a policy.

Sage: A wise policy.

Director: The policy of the wise. And shouldn't we all be wise when we can?

Artist: Yes, yes. But what about the times that call for boldness?

Director: Are you saying that then we shouldn't be wise?

Artist: I'm saying that then the wise don't hold sway, if caution is truly the wise one's way.

~ Masterpieces (Artist, Director, Heir)

Director: Artist, what do you seek?

Artist: Who says I'm seeking anything?

Heir: You've found what you were looking for?

Artist: Yes, yes — of course. My art. What are you seeking after?

Heir: Victory, of course.

Director: Victory in the polls?

Heir: What else?

Director: Well, there could be victories in the legislature.

Heir: I want those victories, too.

Director: And when you have those victories, will you be like Artist?

Heir: What do you mean?

Director: Will you stop seeking?

Heir: Oh, but I don't believe Artist has really stopped seeking.

Artist: What do I seek?

Heir: Your masterpiece.

Artist: Bah, I don't believe in masterpieces. Each of my pieces is its own 'masterpiece'.

Heir: According to your standards. But people will judge one of your pieces to be best.

Artist: And what do they know?

Director: Heir, what if, while you're still quite young, the people judge one of your pieces, as it were, to be your best, to be something you'll never equal?

Heir: I'd seek to prove them wrong.

Artist: Ha! Because you don't believe in masterpieces, either?

Heir: Why, no. It's because I intend to have many more than one.

~ Superiority (Artist, Director, Heir, Sage)

Heir: It's not that I'm trying to be superior to others. I just am.

Director: And do you think that will get you elected?

Heir: Yes. The people want the best.

Director: But best at what?

Heir: What do you mean?

Director: If the people were voting for chief chef, they'd want the best chef. No?

Heir: Of course.

Director: Well, what are you best at that the people want?

Heir: Leadership.

Director: Do you have to be superior in order to lead?

Heir: It certainly helps.

Director: What do you need to be superior at?

Heir: You need to be superior at dealing with others.

Director: What does that involve?

Heir: What does it involve? Isn't it obvious?

Director: It doesn't seem obvious to me.

Heir: Artist, is it obvious to you?

Artist: Well, yes.

Heir: Sage?

Sage: I do think it's obvious.

Heir: You see, Director? It's obvious to everyone but you!

Director: If it's so obvious, then why not tell me what it involves?

Heir: Because you know it when you see it. And I don't doubt you've seen.

~ Disillusionment (Artist, Director, Heir, Sage)

Artist: When morning comes, I often feel disillusioned.

Sage: How so, Artist?

Artist: The dreams I spin in the night dispel in the light of day.

Heir: Then you should spin during the day! And I hope you three will stay well past breakfast. We can do some spinning of our own!

Director: How is it, Heir, that with all these people here you find so much time to spend with us?

Heir: Scarcity drives up price. And my guests must learn to wait.

Director: Why will they learn to wait?

Heir: Because they know I'm in living touch with the people.

Director: Yes, you want the people's votes. You want them to believe in you.

Heir: Of course I do.

Director: But what if one day they stop?

Heir: Stop believing in me? Why would they ever do that?

Director: Because you've stopped believing in them.

Heir: Why would I do that?

Director: Why? Oh, I don't know. Disillusionment?

Heir: The only way I'd be disillusioned is if the people turn out to be other than I thought.

Artist: Ha! By that you mean if they don't vote for you.

Heir: Well, there's truth in that. If I believe in them, they should believe in — and vote for — me. Isn't that how it works?

Artist: Maybe that's how it works. But then the question is: Can you believe in them against what you come to know of them — and against what you come to know... of yourself?

~ Kindness (Artist, Director, Heir, Sage)

Artist: Here's one thing I know about those who would vote you into power, Heir. They're looking for success. And that's it.

Director: Success at all costs? Even that of kindness?

Artist: Kindness? Bah.

Heir: What's wrong with kindness?

Artist: I'll tell you what's wrong. Who deserves kindness? Everyone and no one. So stay focused on success, and let kindness sort itself out.

Sage: How can you say that?

Artist: Well, let's look at it this way, Sage. If you're not successful, what power do you have to be kind?

Sage: We always have the power to be kind. Even the most unsuccessful do.

Artist: Really? Okay, let's say that's true. But then is kindness a matter of last resort? Is it for those with nothing left to lose? Is it merely the final power that remains?

Sage: You're just trying to confuse things, Artist.

Artist: Perhaps things will be more clear if we answer this: When should those in power be kind?

Director: Whenever opportunity affords.

Heir: Affords. Yes, Director. That's exactly the point. Never be kind when you can't afford to be.

Artist: Ha! You agree that being kind can leave you broke?

Heir: If I'm kind to the wrong people? Yes.

Sage: And who would the wrong people be?

Heir: My enemies at their worst.

Sage: But what about killing with kindness? Is that no longer something you'd try?

Heir: Oh, Sage. Sometimes there are better, and more honest — ways to kill.

~ Integration (Artist, Director, Heir, Sage)

Director: What does it mean to integrate?

Heir: To combine things so they become a whole.

Director: And you, what will you seek to combine?

Heir: Everyone, all the people.

Artist: What if some of them don't want to combine?

Heir: Why wouldn't they want to combine?

Artist: Haven't you ever heard of an individual?

Heir: Oh, Artist! The whole I'd create is made up of individuals!

Director: What would you call this whole?

Heir: The nation.

Director: And its parts?

Heir: Citizens. What else?

Director: What's wrong with that, Artist? Isn't that how it has to be? Or do you know of another, better way?

Artist: Of course I know of a better way. What if the individual is the whole?

Sage: Yes, but one whole, the individual, can be integrated into another whole, the nation, without ceasing to be whole.

Artist: No, no. When you're integrated into another whole you always become a part. You're no longer a free standing whole.

Sage: And that's what you object to? Becoming a part?

Artist: Of course that's what I object to, Sage! Why don't you?

Sage: Because I like to be a part of things, to play my part. So tell us — why don't you?

Heir: Oh, Artist likes to play his part. But the part he plays is unique. So it sometimes seems to him he's standing all alone — and he likes it that way.

~ Explanations (Artist, Director, Heir, Sage)

Director: What is pith?

Heir: Forceful and concise expression.

Director: Do the voters want pith?

Heir: Yes.

Director: Do they usually get it?

Heir: No.

Director: Will you give it to them?

Heir: Without doubt.

Sage: Yes, but sometimes you need to explain things in many different ways, and in many words, in order to ensure everyone understands.

Heir: Oh, I don't know, Sage. I prefer a simple and clear way, one way, to explain things.

Director: Artist, is that what you aim for in your works?

Artist: Simplicity and clarity? Yes. But I'm not trying to explain things.

Sage: Then what are you trying to do?

Artist: Show things for what they are. The people who can understand will understand and those who can't will explain away what I say.

Heir: Which amounts to dismissing you.

Artist: Yes.

Sage: But why not help explain things to those who don't understand?

Artist: What can I say, Sage? Some things you need to come to on your own.

Heir: That's what I want from my campaign — people coming to me on their own.

Director: Then that will be quite a campaign. Maybe Artist can depict it in one of his works.

Artist: Ha! You want me to immortalize Heir? Well... why not?

- Immortality (Artist, Director, Heir, Sage)

Heir: Do the immortals truly understand themselves and their fame?

Artist: Themselves? Sometimes. Their fame? Rarely.

Heir: Well, I know myself. And when my fame comes I want to understand.

Artist: Yes, yes — but it's like trying walk forward while looking back at your shadow.

Heir: Then I'll walk away from the sun so I can see my shadow in front of me.

Director: You mean you won't lead the people toward the light?

Heir: Well....

Sage: What's the sun in our metaphor, anyway?

Artist: The goal that creates the shadow of fame.

Sage: But then it makes no difference if you face the sun or not. Your shadow is the same.

Heir: Yes, and as the sun goes down your shadow grows longer.

Director: You'd be proud to have a long shadow?

Heir: If the shadow stands for fame? Yes, of course!

Director: But isn't your shadow just as long when the sun first comes up?

Heir: True. So I need to be present both at sunrise and sunset.

Director: And when the sunrise comes will you lead the people toward the light? Or will you still be fascinated by your own shadow, and look the other way?

Heir: I'll lead them toward the light. But my shadow will grow less as we proceed.

Sage: So if you want the maximum fame, what should you do?

Heir: Lead only at the beginning and end of the day. But that means I'd have to change course from east to west. Not everyone would follow a reversal like that.

Director: Then what must you do?

Heir: Decide which way is more beautiful — and lead only that way.

~ Manners (Artist, Director, Heir, Sage)

Sage: People will follow Heir, in part, because he has beautiful manners.

Director: By beautiful do you mean good?

Sage: I mean Heir is unfailingly polite.

Artist: But what does it mean to be polite?

Sage: To be respectful and considerate of others, Artist.

Artist: But we can split them up.

Sage: What do you mean?

Artist: Respect and consideration are two different things.

Heir: How so?

Artist: I can respect you but not be very considerate toward you.

Heir: True, though unusual. And I suppose you could be considerate but not respect me.

Artist: Exactly.

Sage: But why would someone split these things up? It makes no sense.

Artist: It makes no sense to you because you're not used to considering all the possibilities.

Director: Are you saying Sage lacks imagination?

Artist: Ha! I am.

Sage: Well, let me tell you what I imagine. I imagine the wise have no use for dividing consideration from respect.

Heir: Even when dealing with enemies?

Sage: Even then.

Heir: Why?

Sage: Because the wise have no time for sending out mixed messages. And they don't want their enemies sending them the same.

~ Good (Artist, Director, Heir, Sage)

Artist: The good? What can we possibly say about that that hasn't been said?

Director: Why do we have to say something that hasn't been said?

Heir: Yes. So tell us, Artist — what's been said?

Artist: The good is like the light of the sun.

Sage: But we just said the light of the sun produces fame.

Artist: Are you denying fame is good?

Heir: No, of course he isn't.

Director: But is fame always good?

Heir: Always? Well, I can think of times when fame might be bad. It won't be for me, of course. But I can see how it might be for others.

Director: Is there anything that's always good?

Heir: Yes. Victory, any victory, however small — accompanied by the love of true friends.

Artist: Why can't victory be good on its own, without the love of friends?

Heir: Because then it's hollow.

Artist: Oh, I don't know about that. Suppose a boy goes to a new school. He's yet to make any friends. Then suppose he fights a bully and wins. Wouldn't that be good?

Heir: Of course it would — because it would win him friends!

Sage: Heir has a point. And it holds the other way, too. If the bully had won that wouldn't be good — because bullies always lack true friends.

Director: So what happens if both sides to a fight have an equal love of true friends?

Sage: Both sides are true? They wouldn't fight.

Artist: Ha! Of course they would! It happens all the time. Think about war. There's almost always love and friendship on both sides. And the stronger and more equal the friendship and love, the greater the blood that flows.

- Self-Reliance (Artist, Director, Heir, Sage)

Artist: In the end, we rely on ourselves.

Sage: Oh, but that's not true. In the end, we rely on others.

Artist: For what?

Sage: What do we rely on ourselves for?

Artist: Everything!

Sage: We can rely on others for everything, too.

Artist: This is absurd. Tell us, how do we rely on others?

Sage: We count on them.

Artist: We count! Ha! And what if we miscount?

Sage: You mean they let us down? We forgive, and take things up where we left off.

Artist: Bah. That's when we learn to count on ourselves. And then it's in our power to never let ourselves down.

Heir: But is it?

Artist: Don't tell me you're falling for this nonsense.

Heir: Don't I have to count on the voters?

Artist: Yes, yes — but you count on yourself to win them over.

Director: So why can't it be both? Count on the voters and count on yourself.

Heir: Yes, I like that. Always counting. Always calculating.

Sage: No, Heir, counting doesn't mean to calculate.

Heir: Sure it does! Counting is a simple kind of calculation.

Sage: Yes, but we're not just talking about counting votes. We're talking about reliance, true reliance.

Heir: Of course, Sage. But when I've fully calculated, I'll rely. And things will turn out much better that way.

~ Necessity (Artist, Director, Heir, Sage)

Heir: What's the one thing necessary?

Artist: That all good things must come to an end.

Sage: That we believe in each other.

Director: That we admit when we don't know.

Heir: Only Artist named something necessary.

Sage: Yes, but there's necessary, and then there's necessary.

Heir: You mean necessary if there's to be such-and-such? So what's your such-and-such?

Sage: It's necessary to believe in each other if we're to lead a beautiful life.

Heir: And Director, what's your such-and-such?

Director: It's necessary to admit when we don't know if we're to find the truth.

Heir: I like Director's necessity best.

Sage: But why? Is truth more important than beauty?

Heir: Truth can tell us what's beautiful. But beauty can deceive.

Sage: But then it's not true beauty.

Artist: Why not?

Sage: Because the beautiful is good, and the good never deceives.

Artist: Never? Ha!

Sage: You may laugh, Artist, but I'd go further. I'd say goodness, truth, and beauty are one. And I expect Director agrees.

Director: If what you say is so, then badness, falsehood, and ugliness are one?

Heir: Yes, Director, of course. But do you agree?

Director: Well, before I can answer I need to know if truth is ever ugly. If so, that wrecks the whole point. So let's look to truth, and honestly say what we see.

~ Hopes (Artist, Director, Heir, Sage)

Director: And so the last of the guests are leaving. Have you accomplished what you hoped to accomplish?

Heir: I have. I raised lots of money and gave my campaign its start.

Sage: I'm amazed you don't look the least bit tired. I'm exhausted. This is the longest party I've ever seen.

Heir: Yes, but the marathon is just beginning for me.

Director: And the goal of the marathon is to win the election?

Heir: Why do you ask? Isn't it obvious what the goal is?

Director: Obvious? Perhaps. But you have higher hopes.

Heir: Of course I do.

Director: Isn't it dangerous to hope beyond what you're trying to achieve at the moment?

Heir: Dangerous, sure. But necessary if I'm to achieve my highest hope. I need to lay the groundwork.

Artist: That's the secret to every success. Laying the groundwork.

Sage: Even with your art?

Artist: Of course with my art! What do you think I do? Build without a foundation?

Director: Yes, but I wonder what Heir is hoping to build.

Artist: A name for himself. What else?

Director: Ah, but that can be the most dangerous structure of all.

Heir: How?

Director: You might be tempted to build too fast and too far, so that you risk collapse.

Heir: Then I have no better reason to heed the advice of my good and careful friends! So let's have some coffee — and start drawing up the plans.

Printed in the United States
By Bookmasters